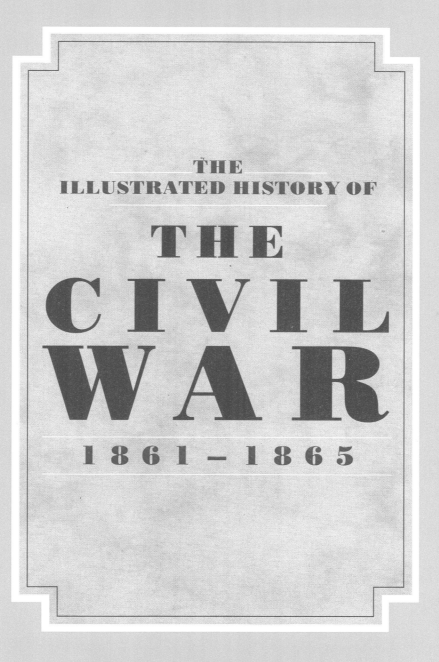

THE
ILLUSTRATED HISTORY OF

THE
CIVIL
WAR

1861 – 1865

ACKNOWLEDGMENT

The author wishes to acknowledge the kindness of Stephen Davis of
Atlanta, Georgia, and Albert Castel of Kalamazoo, Michigan, scholars
and gentlemen, who read the manuscript and offered helpful criticism.

DESIGN	Design Box Ltd., London
EDITOR	David Gibbon
COMMISSIONING EDITOR	Andrew Preston
PICTURE RESEARCH	Leora Kahn
	Meredith Greenfield
ILLUSTRATIONS	Bettmann Archives, New York
	National Archives, Washington, D.C.
	Colour Library Books Ltd.

CLB 2472
© 1992 Colour Library Books Ltd., Godalming, Surrey, England
First published in the United States 1992 by SMITHMARK Publishers Inc.,
16 East 32nd Street, New York, NY 10016
Printed and bound in Singapore by Tien Wah Press
ISBN 0 8317 0775 5

SMITHMARK books are available for bulk purchase for sales
promotion and premium use. For details write or call the
manager of special sales, SMITHMARK Publishers Inc.,
16 East 32nd Street, New York, NY 10016; (212) 532-6600

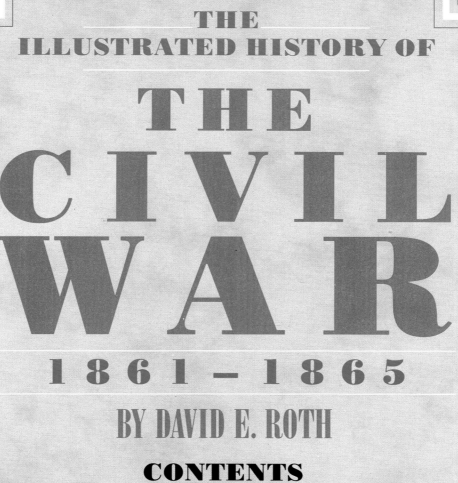

THE ILLUSTRATED HISTORY OF
THE CIVIL WAR
1861 – 1865

BY DAVID E. ROTH

CONTENTS

SMITHMARK

INTRODUCTION

A large country with vast territories yet untamed, a nation with sections that differed in climate, economy and attitudes about government, and a nation of fiercely independent people: that was the United States in the 19th century. Clash was inevitable – predestined – as this young country in the international arena emerged from a New World wilderness to a new world power. In the North, there was rapid industrialization. In the South, an agricultural economy based largely on cotton, with a plantation system and slave labor, remained dominant.

There were divisions even within the chief geographical areas of North and South. In the Northeast, principally New York, Pennsylvania and in the New England states, were the intellectual and moralist leaders – the "very civilized" as it were, the philosophers of the day. And there "too were the cultural and chief financial centers of the young country. Money talked. West of the Allegheny Mountains and the Ohio River were the northern tier of states carved from the wilderness: Ohio, Indiana, Illinois, Wisconsin, Michigan, part of Minnesota. They were not among the original 13 colonies, and because these states were the offspring of the great American experiment in democracy, people of this region were particularly prideful of and loyal to the Union of states.

Below the Mason-Dixon Line – the generally accepted boundary between North and South – the heavy cotton-producing states of the Deep South differed in attitude and outlook from states of the Upper South, where slavery was not as predominant. The population of the Upper South was less than 30 percent slaves, while in the Deep South slaves accounted for almost half the population (47 percent), and over half in the States of Mississippi (55 percent) and South Carolina (57 percent). Diverse interests, diverse attitudes. The situation was volatile as the mid-19th century approached.

As new states entered the Union the question was: slave or free? From this controversy came Fugitive Slave Laws, the Compromise of 1850, the Kansas-Nebraska Act (which gave rise to the violent era known as "Bleeding Kansas"), the Dred Scott Decision, and a host of other legislative and judicial measures designed to quell growing sectional unrest over slavery, but that generally led to more bitterness. Tossed into the mix of debate was the question of state rights versus a strong central government, and even whether the western railroad expansion should be from Northern or Southern cities.

Two events of the late 1850s helped force matters from the political arena to the battlefield. In October 1859, the fanatical abolitionist, John Brown, came east from Kansas and attempted to foment a slave uprising in northern Virginia by seizing the Federal armory at Harpers Ferry. He failed miserably, for many reasons, not the least of which was the fact that slavery was a soft issue in the region. United States troops under Colonel Robert E. Lee took Brown into custody. He was tried and sentenced to hang by a Virginia court. Among the crowd that gathered to watch the execution, which gave the abolitionist movement a martyr, was a young actor named Booth, who this day wore a borrowed uniform of the Virginia militia, but who would one day don the cloak of an assassin.

The second development that brought the nation closer to war was the rise of the Republican party, which emerged from the split within the Democratic party over slavery and the right of states to govern themselves. The election of Abraham Lincoln, the Republican candidate, in November 1860, was considered by the Deep South to be a victory for abolition, a strong central government, and Northern financial interests. As a result, on December 20, the State of South Carolina declared its ties with the Union dissolved. Compromise had failed. A nation moved toward war.

A portrait of President Lincoln, who stood for much that the South hated, but not everything that the radical Republican Abolitionists wanted.

1861

The first quarter of the year was one of great uncertainty, apprehension, and political double-crossing. It became a test of wills early on as the State of South Carolina plucked its star from the flag of the United States and declared itself an independent nation, demanding that the Federal government relinquish all claims to military facilities in the state. Focus became centered on Fort Sumter in the middle of Charleston Harbor, where Major Robert Anderson and his small Federal garrison were pawns in a political chess game of impending civil war. Anderson and his men, not more than 120 in number, including 34 civilian workmen, had been holed up in the fort since the day after Christmas, after moving from nearby Fort Moultrie on Sullivan's Island, which had been deemed too vulnerable to assault from the mainland. The garrison had not been supplied or reinforced, and its

forces, cautioned against resupplying the fort under armed escort. Send a merchant vessel, a very fast one, Scott advised. It wasn't as threatening.

Tensions mounted everywhere. In Georgia, militia troops took over the high-walled, moated Fort Pulaski, which guarded the sea route to the waterfront of old Savannah. Also, the nation's capital, nestled squarely in the lap of secessionist sympathy, was said to be in peril of invasion by marauders. Federal arsenals at Mount Vernon, Alabama, and Apalachicola, Florida, were declared properties of those respective states, though both were still in the Union. Then, on January 9, Mississippi seceded, followed over the next two days by Florida and Alabama, then Georgia on the 19th, Louisiana on the 26th, and Texas on February 1. These were the states of the Deep South, where King Cotton ruled, and where the Federal threat to

capacity to wage war, even to defend itself, dwindled with each passing day, while the "enemy's" grew, as the Carolinians ringed the harbor with guns and fortifications.

If the hapless Sumter garrison looked to Washington for help, the men soon realized that the lame duck occupant of the White House, James Buchanan, wanted nothing more than for the final days of his term to slip away rapidly and without incident. Let the president-elect sort out the mess, Buchanan reasoned. After all, was it not the election of Abraham Lincoln that had sparked the whole crisis of secession? If Buchanan attempted to supply and reinforce Fort Sumter, it could be just the impetus needed for the "Fire-eaters" in South Carolina to claim an act of war. General Winfield Scott, 73 years old, obese, and chief of all United States

the region's economy and way of life loomed greatest.

Meanwhile, President Buchanan was plagued by double-dealing in his own cabinet. The fast merchant vessel recommended by General Scott, *Star of the West,* had left New York for Fort Sumter on January 5. News of its departure and mission reached South Carolina through the offices of Jacob Thompson, a Mississippian who was also Secretary of the Interior in Buchanan's shaky cabinet. Thompson tele-graphed Charleston that *Star of the West* was on its way with troops and supplies for Fort Sumter, then he resigned his cabinet post and headed south. This incident followed close on the heels of the resignation of Secretary of War John B. Floyd, a Virginian by birth and alumnus of South Carolina College. He had

Fort Sumter as seen from the South Carolina shore batteries. The garrison, under Major Robert Anderson, surrendered within a few hours.

apparently attempted to aid the Southern Cause by stockpiling ordnance in Southern-based installations which, presumably, would soon be seized by the secessionists. Floyd resigned his powerful cabinet position on December 29. Five days later the War Department cancelled one of Floyd's orders to ship guns south from a Pittsburgh arsenal. The country was falling apart.

When *Star of the West* steamed into Charleston Harbor on the morning of January 9, a battery on Morris Island let loose with a salvo. The message was all too clear. It didn't matter whether supplies came by warship or merchant vessel or rowboat. Any attempt to assist the Fort Sumter garrison, according to South Carolina Governor Francis Pickens, would be considered an act of war.

On February 4, a convention of the seven seceded states met at the Alabama state capitol in Montgomery and organized a provisional government called the Confederate States of America. After five days of debate, Jefferson Davis, a former U.S. Senator from Mississippi and one-time Secretary of War (who neither sought nor relished a post in the fledgling government of the South), became provisional president. Georgia's Alexander H. "Little Aleck" Stephens (he reputedly weighed a scant 90 pounds) was selected as vice president. Neither man was considered a radical secessionist, or "Fire-eater," so choosing them to head the government seemed to be intended to appeal to the Upper South states, which were still sitting on the secession fence. It was still a game of politics. No one had been killed yet.

Abraham Lincoln, after avoiding alleged plots to kill him in Baltimore, while en route to Washington from his Illinois home, was inaugurated as the 16th President of the United States on March 4. Lincoln pledged in his inaugural address not to interfere with slavery where it existed. Furthermore, he declared the secession ordinances of the seven departed states null and void, because it was uncon-stitutional to attempt the dissolution of the Union. And he challenged his "dissatisfied fellow countrymen" in the South that the onus of civil war, should it come, would be upon their shoulders, not the new administration's. Reaction from the South was quick and sharp. Every word of Lincoln's address was construed as nothing short of a declaration of war.

War was not long in coming. On March 29, Lincoln pledged to save Fort Sumter, as well as pledging aid for threatened Fort Pickens at Pensacola, Florida. Three warships and a revenue cutter prepared to sail. On April 6, official notification of the relief expedition was made to Governor Pickens, who now shared the leadership limelight at Charleston with General Pierre Gustave Toutant Beauregard, the recently appointed commander of all Confederate military forces in the area. All of Charleston and its harbor environs were placed on military alert.

On the 11th a formal demand for the surrender of Fort Sumter was made to Major Anderson by three emissaries under a white flag of truce. He attempted to skirt the surrender issue by stating he'd soon be starved out, so why resort to armed aggression? The three Confederates weren't prepared for this sort of response, so they rowed back to the mainland to confer with higher officials. By eleven o'clock that night they were back at Fort Sumter, asking Anderson just how long it would be before he was starved out. The major left them waiting for two and a half hours while he thought it over. His answer: the 15th – he'd evacuate the fort at noon on the 15th of April. That was totally unacceptable. Everyone knew a relief expedition was on its way and would surely arrive before the 15th. The emissaries put Anderson on notice that guns would open on him in one hour. At 4:30 a.m., April 12, 1861, the guns opened, and the American Civil War exploded into headlines worldwide.

After a 34-hour bombardment, which occasionally turned into a duel, whenever the garrison engaged in limited return fire (none of which was targeted at Charleston itself, so as not to injure civilians), Major Anderson, at about two-thirty on the afternoon of April 13, ran up a white surrender flag. Meanwhile, the relief expedition had arrived at the harbor mouth, but dared go no further. The ships watched helplessly as Fort Sumter was pounded, then they steamed away with all the supplies. Anderson formally surrendered the fort in a ceremony on the 14th, which cost the life of one soldier when a salute gun exploded. He was the only casualty of the opening engagement of the war.

On April 15, President Lincoln called for 75,000 volunteers to put down the insurrection. States in the Upper South thought his actions were too rash and uncalculated in the circumstances. Talk of secession conventions became rampant, and before the month was out Virginia – the Old Dominion – had cast its lot with the new Confederacy, followed in May by Arkansas and North Carolina, and Tennessee in June. Young men answered the call of their states, North and South, and fields, shops and factories emptied as military ranks swelled with youthful bravado, everyone eager for fighting and glory. Many predicted it would all be over soon – one big battle would settle it – and no one wanted to miss out.

Washington was in turmoil. It seemed as if no worse place could have been found for the nation's capital. Across the Potomac River was Virginia, just seceded from the Union. Surrounding the capital on its other sides was Maryland, a state seething with secessionist sympathies to the point that a firefight had broken out between armed citizens and Massachusetts troops who were marching through Baltimore on their way to Washington. About a dozen people lost their lives in the Baltimore Riot of April 19, which was finally quelled by force of

arms. Lincoln placed the city under martial law for the rest of the war.

Old General Scott had complained on numerous occasions of the inadequate Regular Army of the United States, with hardly enough men in uniform (fewer than 20,000) for peacetime necessities, let alone in time of national crisis. His opinion was justified as Lincoln looked upon his legions of green warriors fresh from New England shops and Pennsylvania farms and the backwoods of the Midwest, marching to and fro with phony guns and laughable order, trying to learn how to be soldiers. But sufficient time was not at hand to allow these boys proper training. Rebel forces (just as untrained) under Generals Joseph E. Johnston and Beauregard, the latter having been relocated from South Carolina, posed a real threat in Virginia. Johnston was in the strategic Shenandoah Valley, a perfect invasion corridor aimed at Washington that would become a constant battleground of the war, while Beauregard's force was at Manassas, not three dozen miles from the Federal capital city.

Union General Irvin McDowell was prodded to deal with the threat. Exasperated by meddling politicians and the urgency of public opinion, he finally set his army in motion long before it was properly trained and organized. They met the Rebels along Bull Run, near Manassas, on July 21. McDowell's plan was well thought out: defeat Beauregard before he could join forces with Johnston. But luck was against McDowell, for Johnston's men arrived in time to turn the tide of battle. It was a very confused clash, often characterized as a battle between two mobs, as the inexperience of both armies was all too evident. To make matters worse, some Confederate units wore blue uniforms, and some Federal units wore gray, and the two

sides had flags so similar in color and features that after the battle the Confederates designed a new, more distinctive one. The Confederates won this first significant engagement of the war, and one commander, Thomas J. Jackson, earned the nickname "Stonewall," ironically for a defensive stand his men had made, when Jackson's forte would prove to be lightning marches and audacious attacks. The Yankees were swept from the field in an embarrassing retreat that literally overran picnickers and other curious sorts who had come out to the country from Washington to witness the battle.

After the Battle of Manassas, or Bull Run as it was called in the North, both sides settled into a period of fortifying, training and stockpiling supplies, as the realization dawned on everyone that this would not be a quick, one-battle war. The Confederates, heartened by their recent victory, moved as close to Washington as Centreville, astride one of the main roads to the capital, but still a respectful distance away. Southern spirits were lifted even higher in August when news arrived of a victory at Wilson's Creek in Missouri, in which the Union commander, General Nathaniel Lyon, was killed.

The North, stinging from defeat and humiliation, nevertheless was stronger in its commitment to avenge the losses and preserve the Union. General Scott, known as "Old Fuss and Feathers," was quietly shelved as an old soldier well past his prime. He was replaced by the swaggering, 34-year-old General George B. McClellan, who had enjoyed minor successes in western Virginia. At the time, though, they seemed like monumental victories in light of other events. McClellan, known as "Little Mac" or, as time went by, the "Young Napoleon," set about drilling and refitting his command, which was called the Army of the Potomac, and generally bragging

Legions of young volunteers, "green warriors," swapped the comforts of home for the rough and ready lifestyle of the soldier.

himself into an inflated status that even he began to believe was true, but which he would prove incapable of fulfilling.

West of the Alleghenies, Confederates under General Leonidas Polk, who wore the robes of an Episcopal Bishop when not soldiering, violated Kentucky's neutrality in early September by marching into Columbus and erecting a stronghold high on bluffs overlooking the Mississippi River. A few miles upriver, at Cairo, Illinois, where the Ohio River met the Mississippi, General Ulysses S. Grant commanded a small Federal force. In response to Polk's occupation of Columbus, Grant, on September 6, seized Paducah, Kentucky, at the confluence of the Tennessee and Ohio rivers.

The following November, Grant dropped down the Mississippi with his men on steamboats to test the Columbus defenses. The result was the Battle of Belmont, Missouri, fought opposite the Columbus fortifications, during which Grant's men seized a Rebel camp and plundered it before Polk's main force could respond from across the river. The battle was a learning experience for the men and officers of both sides, and it even turned comical as Grant became one of the last men back on the transports after playing a dangerous game of hide-and-seek with pursuing Confederates. Grant never forgot this early battlefield escapade, when his men lost control of themselves and nearly met disaster.

This ten-dollar note was one of the first types issued by the Confederate Treasury. The Confederate currency diminished rapidly in value as the war progressed.

In command of Confederate forces in the West was General Albert Sidney Johnston. He had the unenviable task of holding a vast expanse of territory with inadequate numbers of troops. Johnston attempted to set up a defense in Kentucky, with Tennessee to his back. His line consisted of various forts and installations stretching from the Mississippi River "Gibraltar" at Columbus, through Bowling Green on the Barren River in south-central Kentucky, thence eastward to Cumberland Gap in the mountains on the border with Virginia. Two rivers cut through Kentucky as potential invasion routes into Tennessee,

so to defend these waterways the Confederacy built Fort Henry on the Tennessee River and Fort Donelson on the Cumberland River. Both of these forts were in northern Tennessee, near the Kentucky line, and had been sited before Kentucky's neutrality was violated. To be sure, the forts were not placed in optimum locations, but work had already begun on them, time was of the essence, and the Confederates had to make the best of what they had.

The inadequacy of Johnston's line, as well as the incompetence of some of the officers under him, was made all too clear only 19 days into the new year.

*Ulysses S. Grant, whose early victories – some of them close-run – gave
the people of the North the hero that they had been looking for.*

Confederate General Felix Zollicoffer, an influential newspaperman with little military experience, led a force of about 4,000 men out of the mountain protection of Cumberland Gap to a precarious position, with their backs to the Cumberland River, at a place called Mill Springs, or Logan Crossroads. There he was soundly whipped by a force under General George H. Thomas in a battle that cost Zollicoffer his life. For the Union, the nation's confidence in the Western troops was strengthened, and pro-Confederate sympathies in Kentucky, a state severely divided in loyalties, was weakened.

Then, in rapid succession, U.S. Grant's forces, which included the river navy of Flag Officer Andrew H. Foote, captured Forts Henry and Donelson (on February 6 and 16, respectively). The Confederates had no choice but to evacuate Bowling Green and their Columbus fortifications, and then Nashville, the Tennessee capital city, was occupied by Federal forces without resistance on February 25. By June the Federals even held Cumberland Gap. Further west, across the Mississippi in northwestern Arkansas, near the border with Missouri, Confederate forces under General Earl Van Dorn were defeated in the two-day battle of Pea Ridge, March 7-8, dashing their hopes of reestablishing a Confederate foothold in Missouri. Like Kentucky, Missouri was an important border state much divided in loyalties.

On April 6, Albert Sidney Johnston tried a similar attempt to regain territory by launching a surprise attack from his base in northern Mississippi against Grant's troops camped along the Tennessee River in southwestern Tennessee. Fighting was desperate around Shiloh Church and the Yankees were pushed back steadily on the 6th, but, reinforced during the night, Grant managed to win the day on the 7th. The Battle of Shiloh was a close call for the emerging Union hero of the West, and with combined casualties of nearly 24,000 in the two-day struggle, including General Johnston, who bled to death on the field, the battle proved to both sides that this was not only to be a long war, but a very bloody one too.

Thus, the year 1862 opened with Union successes in the Western Theater, some of which were strategically decisive, and witnessed the emergence of Ulysses S. Grant, a man so humble and full of self-doubt at the beginning of the war that he was certain no one would give him a command of any significance.

One of the principal strategies of the Union was a blockade of Southern ports and the splitting of the Confederacy by seizing control of the Mississippi River. Grant's success in Kentucky and Tennessee contributed in no small degree to opening the Mississippi by loosening the Confederacy's grip on these vital areas. On March 14, Union General John Pope captured New Madrid, Missouri, and laid siege to nearby Island Number 10 in the Mississippi, which finally fell on April 7. By June the Federal fleet captured Memphis after a spectacular naval battle, complete with rammings and broadsides at close quarters, all of which was observed with intense interest and growing disappointment by folks lining the Memphis waterfront.

Operating against the other end of the river was a huge fleet of warships, mortar boats and infantry transports under Admiral David G. Farragut, which began bombarding Forts Jackson and St. Philip below New Orleans on April 18. A week later Farragut landed at New Orleans, reclaiming it in the name of the United States of America. And so began a long and oftentimes harsh, sometimes humorous, occupation of the Confederacy's largest city. Now

Fort Donelson, and fifteen thousand prisoners, were captured by the troops of U.S. Grant on the afternoon of February 16, 1862.

only Vicksburg was an obstacle to the Union's complete control of the "Father of Waters." (Later, though, the Confederates fortified Port Hudson, making it an additional obstacle to Union domination of the Mississippi River.)

On the East Coast, the modern age of naval warfare was ushered in with the first clash of ironclad vessels as the USS *Monitor* and CSS *Virginia* (formerly USS *Merrimack*) battled to a stalemate at Hampton Roads, near Norfolk, Virginia. Elsewhere along the Atlantic coast, Federal troops under General Ambrose E. Burnside made amphibious landings on the North Carolina shoreline and pushed inland and along the coast, seizing the port city of New Bern on March 14, and capturing Fort Macon on April 25, after a month-long siege. The capture of Fort Macon, coupled with the seizure of Fort Pulaski near Savannah on April 11, spelled the doom of medieval-style forts as a means of defense. Once thought impregnable, the moated, high-walled brick forts had been no match for the improved, long-range, heavy rifled artillery brought to bear on them. The big guns blasted huge holes in both forts, forcing their surrender. Lessons were many, and hard-learned, in these early days of the war.

In contrast to the brilliant successes of Union forces in the West, General McClellan's Army of the Potomac turned in a dismal record for 1862. Constantly prodded by Lincoln to do something at least threatening in the direction of the Confederates, still encamped at Centreville, not far from the capital, Little Mac seemed content to drill and organize and drill some more, to the point that on March 11, he was demoted from General-in-Chief of all Federal armies (Scott's old job) to commander of just the Department and Army of the Potomac, still an enormous responsibility. When McClellan did get around to moving, he moved ponderously, giving "chase" to the retreating Confederate army of Joe Johnston as it fell back from Centreville to a new and presumably better position on the Rappahannock River.

"On to Richmond!" became the battle cry of the Army of the Potomac. When the Confederates in May 1861 relocated their seat of government to the Virginia capital of Richmond, a scant 100 miles south of Washington, it was predestined that the intervening ground would become blood-soaked before the war ended. But in his first major offensive, McClellan's approach was not overland, but seaward. In devising the Peninsula Campaign, he turned his back on Johnston's army in northern Virginia. Instead of a direct confrontation, McClellan loaded his massive army on transports for a trip by way of the Potomac River and Chesapeake Bay to Union-held Fortress Monroe, on the tip of the peninsula between the York and James rivers.

It was a tremendous undertaking, but the transfer of 100,000 men, bag and baggage, with horses, mules and wagons, artillery, and supplies, was immaculately executed by McClellan, the master planner, and by April 5, he was laying siege to Yorktown and its 15,000 defenders. Nearly a month later he was still sitting before Yorktown, pleading for reinforcements, though he never held worse than a two-to-one edge over the Confederates during the whole campaign. Little Mac's delays allowed Johnston to bring his army down from the Rappahannock line.

In order to hold the attention of Union forces in northern Virginia after Johnston's relocation, and to prevent reinforcements from being sent to McClellan, Confederates under Stonewall Jackson in the Shenandoah Valley created a strategic diversion that has been heralded as one of the most brilliant operations in military history. The enigmatic Jackson, who was extremely religious, sucked on lemons, and told no one of his plans, and his legendary "foot cavalry," managed in a series of lightning marches and surprise attacks to create the illusion of much greater numbers, and in so doing, in one month's time, tramped some 350 miles, fought five battles (McDowell on May 8, Front Royal on May 23, Winchester on the 25th, Cross Keys on June 8, and Port Republic on the 9th), in which three different Union armies were defeated, inflicted twice their own number of casualties, even though outnumbered two-to-one, or worse, and managed to hold the attention of an estimated 60,000 potential re-inforcements for McClellan. Jackson's Shenandoah Valley Campaign is one of the most remarkable and fascinating episodes of a war filled with human interest and drama.

Once McClellan finally got his army moving on the Peninsula, he made good gains, entering an evacuated Yorktown on May 3. Pushing the Rebels out of Williamsburg on the 5th, by the end of the month the church steeples of Richmond were in sight. There Johnston finally turned to lash back at the pressing Federals, who were at the moment vulnerable, straddling the Chickahominy River east of Richmond. In the ensuing Battle of Seven Pines (or Fair Oaks), fought May 31-June 1, Johnston was severely wounded on the first day of the fight. He was replaced by President Davis' military advisor, General Robert E. Lee, who had thus far in the war racked up a string of failures in minor engagements in mountainous western Virginia, and had performed routine inspections of coastal installations along the Atlantic seaboard. The change in command would prove momentous.

It turned out that Lee had been the mastermind behind the Shenandoah Valley diversion, so ably executed by Stonewall Jackson. Their relationship would grow, for even the secretive Stonewall trusted Lee, and perhaps no one else. The Battle of Seven Pines ended in stalemate, and McClellan's army remained lurking on the outskirts of the Confederate capital. Lee went on the offensive. In a series of battles known as the Seven Days, June 25-July 1, Robert E. Lee began to emerge as the premier commander of the South (a transformation that

would reach fruition during the ensuing Second Manassas Campaign).

Skirmishing on June 25 proved indecisive. Meanwhile, Stonewall Jackson's men arrived from the Shenandoah Valley to reinforce Lee. The next day the Confederates struck hard at Mechanicsville, pushing back a portion of McClellan's huge and divided army. On the 27th, the Battle of Gaines' Mill was another offensive by the Army of Northern Virginia, which saw Federals again in retreat. At Savage Station on the 29th, McClellan's rear guard was struck, forcing him to leave behind nearly 3,000 sick and wounded men. The Battle of Frayser's Farm (or White Oak Swamp) on June 30 was a confused fight in which Lee attempted a double-strike from the north and west through a desolate swamp. Nothing went right, but the mere audacity of the Confederates kept Little Mac on alert and moving backward. Lee's campaign to save the capital ended on the seventh day of fighting, July 1, at Malvern Hill. The ill-advised attacks in this battle were extremely costly for Lee and drew severe criticism. But it was still early in the war, everyone was learning, and Lee had indeed saved Richmond.

The next phase of fighting in the Eastern Theater was the Second Manassas (or Bull Run) Campaign. The three forces of Union troops so roughly handled by Stonewall Jackson in the Shenandoah were subsequently consolidated and styled the Army of Virginia. It was placed under General John Pope, just arrived from the West, where he had enjoyed success. Pope's boasts rankled nearly everyone, and his harsh treatment of civilians in northern Virginia earned him the undying enmity of someone in a position to get back at him, Robert E. Lee.

With McClellan's army still on the Peninsula below Richmond, Pope's mission was to march into Virginia and create a new front for the Confederates to contend with. Jackson had since joined Lee for the Seven Days (during which Stonewall was criticized for being too slow). Nevertheless, with Jackson out of the way, Pope had ample space in which to operate. He started marching on July 14. In response, Lee demonstrated his contempt for McClellan, who was sitting largely inactive at his new base on the James River, by dispatching Jackson northward, soon followed by General A.P. Hill's troops, and eventually Lee's whole army.

The same northward shift soon occurred in McClellan's army, with significant consequences to Little Mac and the whole command structure. As units arrived back in Washington they were funnelled out to Pope and thus taken from McClellan's control. The resulting battles of Cedar Mountain (August 9), Groveton (August 28), Second Manassas (August 29-30), and Chantilly (September 1) constituted the one and only campaign of the short-lived Army of Virginia. Pope was soundly whipped by Lee's army, and the Yankees were sent scurrying, again, for the Washington defenses.

Lincoln then made an important command decision. Lee had to be stopped; Confederates were again in position to threaten the capital. Despite not leading them to any great victories, McClellan was adored by most of his troops. Because of the current emergency he seemed the best choice. The Army of Virginia was dissolved, and McClellan resumed command of an even heftier Army of the Potomac. But what about Pope? Conveniently, during August the Sioux Indians had gotten restless in Minnesota and were killing people. Off went Pope to Minnesota, shelved for one defeat, but mostly because of his irritating personality.

Survivors of the 51st New York Infantry pose reflectively for this photograph after the Battle of Second Manassas (or Bull Run), August 29-30, 1862.

Late summer of 1862 saw three northward thrusts by the Confederates, none of which were successful. In early September, Lee raided north into Maryland and came close to disaster. His plans had fallen into enemy hands, but the "enemy" was McClellan, who reacted predictably slowly, but he still managed to place Lee in a perilous situation with a huge Union army bearing down on the dangerously divided Confederate forces. Sharp fighting at South Mountain on September 14 held off the approaching Army of the Potomac long enough for Stonewall Jackson to capture Harpers Ferry on the 15th. This allowed Lee to concentrate his army for a stand along Antietam Creek, at Sharpsburg, Maryland.

The battle there on September 17 was the bloodiest single day in American history, with some 24,000 casualties in blue and gray – all Americans. McClellan failed to smash Lee's much smaller army, but did force the Confederate leader to retreat back into Virginia, thus spoiling what ultimately proved to be the Confederacy's best prospects for British recognition. President Lincoln took advantage of the success to issue his Emancipation Proclamation against slavery.

Across the mountains, Confederate Generals Braxton Bragg and Edmund Kirby Smith struck north through Tennessee and Kentucky, nearly to the banks of the Ohio River, before squabbles between the two generals brought the invasion to a standstill. The Battle of Perryville on October 8 ended the otherwise successful invasion. The battle was a stalemate, but Bragg, in order to trace a line of supply, was forced to leave the field to his enemy. Still further west, in Mississippi, a thrust intended to carry Con-federate forces under Earl Van Dorn into western Tennessee was turned back by General William S. Rosecrans at Corinth on October 3-4.

The onset of winter didn't discourage military operations in 1862. At Prairie Grove, Arkansas, on December 7, in the ongoing struggle for control of Missouri – even just a corner of it, in this case the southwest one – Union forces under Generals James G. Blunt and Francis J. Herron defeated Confederates under General Thomas C. Hindman in a battle that produced 2,600 casualties, many of whom froze to death during the night. The dashing and womanizing Earl Van Dorn, whose defeat at Corinth had gotten him demoted to a cavalry commander, launched a successful raid on Grant's supply base at Holly Springs, Mississippi, on December 20. Grant, who was engaged in operations against Vicksburg, lost 1,500 men as prisoners at Holly Springs, and $1.5 million in supplies. Van Dorn regained some of his reputation as a soldier, but it was his reputation as a woman chaser that led to his demise. The following May he was shot and killed by a jealous husband at Spring Hill, Tennessee.

In the Virginia theater, Lincoln finally had all he could stand of McClellan's "slows" after Antietam, and on November 7 replaced him with Ambrose Burnside, who openly expressed doubts about his ability to command such a huge army. He proved himself right at the Battle of Fredericksburg on December 13, where the slaughter of his men in futile attacks was so great that it prompted Lee to contemplate how one might grow too fond of war. In Tennessee, the year ended with fighting on New Year's Eve along the banks of Stones River near Murfreesboro. Union commander William Rosecrans emerged the victor by the narrowest of margins, after a terrible struggle that carried into the new year. Bragg, his opponent, left the field on January 3.

For the Union, the year began and ended with victories in Tennessee. East of the mountains, though, Lee reigned supreme.

At the Battle of Fredericksburg, Burnside's army suffered a total of 12,700 killed and wounded after making repeated frontal assaults on Lee's entrenched positions on the high ground.

The new year opened with Lincoln's Emancipation Proclamation taking effect. For the moment it was largely a useless document as far as the institution of slavery was concerned, but it was packed with political clout on the international front. It caused some upheaval in the armies of the North as soldiers re-evaluated their reasons for fighting – preserving the Union was one thing, an abolitionist crusade was another; there were some desertions among the rank and file. As the document read, slaves in territories still at war with the United States were now called "free," but the Proclamation did not disturb slavery in areas behind Union lines. Still, the moral and psychological impact of the Emancipation Proclamation was hailed internationally as a bold and brilliant stroke for Lincoln, equal to several battlefield victories.

Union generals and their armies, not politicians, would be the great emancipators, conquering territory and thus freeing the slaves therein as the armies marched through. This created huge caravans of blacks trailing behind the Western armies, sometimes slowing the column and always a drain on supplies. Lincoln's proclamation also allowed former slaves to be admitted to the armed forces. Eventually an estimated 200,000 blacks entered Federal service, and Lincoln later claimed their participation contributed significantly to preserving the Union.

Some commanders, such as General William T. Sherman, refused to accept black units, except as garrison troops in rear areas, and he criticized government officials who attempted to recruit black regiments in his department. Late in the war, Sherman even burned a bridge behind him to prevent freed slaves from following his army. Black soldiers were never really accepted as equals by most of their white comrades in arms; their units were officered by whites, and until 1865 they were paid less than whites. Risks were greater in black units, too. The Confederate government decreed that white officers commanding black units were guilty of inciting slave uprisings and thus subject to execution if captured. Black soldiers took great risks too, for they rarely ended up on prisoner lists.

Meanwhile, at Fredericksburg General Burnside was still bringing shame to his Army of the Potomac with a miserable campaign that literally bogged down in the muck and mire of a Virginia winter, entering the history books as "Burnside's Mud March." The general had overstayed his welcome and on January 25 was replaced by General Joseph Hooker, a boastful sort, prime critic of Burnside, and a man who once said the government needed a dictator. To be a dictator, wrote Lincoln to his newest army commander, one needs great victories on the battlefield. Get him those victories and Lincoln would risk the dictatorship.

With the coming of spring Hooker gave all the indications of doing just that by deftly stealing a march on Lee and getting behind him. Then, however, Hooker lost his nerve and allowed the Lee-Jackson team to out-march, out-maneuver and out-general him at the Battle of Chancellorsville, May 1-4, sending the Potomac boys heading for safety behind the Rappahannock River. It was yet another disaster for Union forces in the East. Lee boldly split his army three separate times in the face of a superior foe, and in the end a flanking force under Stonewall Jackson provided the decisive blow. Chancellorsville has been called Lee's greatest victory, though a very costly one. Mighty Stonewall was accidentally wounded by his own men and died of complications on May 10.

Lee reorganized his army from two corps to three, dividing Jackson's old corps between Generals Richard S. Ewell (Second Corps) and A.P. Hill (Third), while James Longstreet retained command of the First Corps. In command of Lee's cavalry was the flamboyant General James Ewell Brown "Jeb" Stuart, whose ride completely around McClellan's army on the Peninsula in '62 had only served to make him more of a risk-taker. Indeed, his horsemen held the upper hand over their Eastern counterparts in blue so far in this war, but times were changing and consequences were more dire now. Lee endured Stuart's antics and flashy dress, knowing how valuable the young cavalryman was in reconnaissance and screening the army. Right now, Stuart was to screen the Army of Northern Virginia as it embarked on its most daring invasion of the North – one that would take them to the lush, unspoiled farmlands of Pennsylvania.

The beginning of the northward thrust was delayed and nearly exposed at its outset when Stuart was caught napping at Brandy Station, Virginia. In his full contempt for the enemy cavalry, Stuart had been lax with the dispositions of his units and in vigilance, allowing General Alfred Pleasonton's Union horsemen to catch him fully unawares on the morning of June 9, the day the northward march was to commence. Only after hard fighting and superb leadership under extreme pressure did Stuart manage a tactical victory in what was the largest cavalry fight on the North American continent. Stuart's men grudgingly accorded a new respect for Yankee cavalry after Brandy Station.

There were several reasons for Lee's invasion of the North. First and foremost, Virginia was trampled and desolate after two years of war. The Old Dominion needed a rest. By moving into Pennsylvania, Lee would relieve pressure on Richmond – where a bread riot had occurred in April – and his army could live off the enemy's land for a change. Further-more, a victory on Yankee soil might garner more support for Northern Peace Democrats, known as "Copperheads." Most of these individuals sought a politically negotiated end to the war through certain concessions to the South, while at

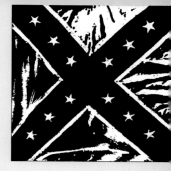

the extreme was the notion to allow the South to go its own way. That same victory might entice European recognition and support.

The Army of Northern Virginia swept northward after Brandy Station with considerable elan, as if possessed by the spirit of the lamented Jackson. On June 14-15, his old command whipped a Federal force under General Robert Milroy at Winchester in the Shenandoah, the Valley veterans' old stomping grounds. By the 24th, Confederates were across the Potomac and on Pennsylvania soil.

There was one problem. The army was spread far and wide for strategic as well as foraging purposes, and Stuart, the "eyes" of Lee's army, was off on another of his daring rides – perhaps trying to erase some of the embarrassment of Brandy Station – leaving Lee's infantry blind in enemy territory. Meanwhile, Hooker had been relieved of command of the Army of the Potomac and replaced by General George G. Meade on June 28. Meade did not possess the overbearing and boastful qualities of past commanders. He was a solid and steady leader. When Lee heard of the change in command, he predicted that Meade would not make the careless mistakes other Yankee commanders had made. The Army of the Potomac gave pursuit and Lee's invasion culminated in a chance meeting at the crossroads town of Gettysburg in south-central Pennsylvania. In three days of desperate fighting, July 1-3, 1863, Meade's army turned back the best the South had to offer in the greatest battle of the war. Over 50,000 casualties resulted, and a turning point in the war was at hand: in addition to the Army of the Potomac's success at Gettysburg, another great Union victory was achieved in the West.

While Lee began his retreat from Gettysburg on July 4, Independence Day, 1863, General U.S.Grant accepted the surrender of Vicksburg, Mississippi, after a lengthy siege. Since early May, Grant had Vicksburg in his sights, with fighting at Port Gibson (May 1), Raymond (May 12), Jackson, the capital of Mississippi (May 14), Champion's Hill (May 16), and at the Big Black River (May 17). These engagements merely got Grant into position before Vicksburg, and the siege began on May 18. Grisly tales came out of Vicksburg after its surrender – families living in caves, the stench of decay (human and animal), people feeding on rats, and the sheer hell of being under bombardment for days. Siege operations were also underway at Port Hudson, Louisiana, lower down on the Mississippi, where the last Rebel garrison on the river held out until July 8. The Union now held the great river from its headwaters in Minnesota to its mouth at the Gulf of Mexico, and thousands of prisoners.

Elsewhere in the South, Union attacks on Fort Wagner near Charleston, South Carolina brought into battle one of the first black units raised in the North, the 54th Massachusetts under Colonel Robert G. Shaw, son of a wealthy Boston abolitionist. The July 18th assault was very costly to the regiment and resulted in the death of Shaw, but failed to take the fort. A month later, on August 17, in a reversal of roles from the opening guns of the war, Union batteries erupted on Confederate-occupied Fort Sumter and fired over 900 shots on Sumter, Fort Wagner and Battery Gregg. The bombardment continued in earnest through the 23rd. After 5,000 rounds, which reduced Fort Sumter's brick walls to rubble and dust, the Confederates miraculously still held out. Sporadic fire continued until the 27th, with still no white flag at Fort Sumter; however, the Confederates evacuated Fort Wagner on Morris Island on September 6.

Two days later, a heroic stand was made by a handful of determined Texans under Lieutenant Dick Dowling, manning a mud fort. They turned back an amphibious invasion force at Sabine Pass, a narrow waterway separating Texas and Louisiana that dumps into the Gulf of Mexico. (The scrappy Texans, mostly Irish, were considerably aided by a sandbar that the Union boats couldn't negotiate.)

In the North, draft riots in New York City claimed lives and property. The summer of 1863 also saw a new star added to the flag of the United States as delegates in western Virginia elected to sever ties with the Old Dominion and to form their own state, West Virginia, loyal to the Union – though loyalties in this new border state remained divided and bushwhacking in the mountains reached a new high. Confederate General John Hunt Morgan raided through Ohio in July with his free-wheeling horsemen and did more damage than good for the Southern cause. The majority of his command was eventually captured, including Morgan himself, and his raid through "Copperhead country" created such a scare that many Peace Democrats converted

Robert E.Lee was the paragon of Southern military heroes. At the start of the war, he already had an enviable military record, and both sides were anxious to secure his services.

to staunch avengers. Three months later they helped elect a strong war governor in Ohio.

In Kansas, Confederate guerrilla William C. Quantrill, a Northerner by birth (Ohio), exercised no manly restraint in an August raid on the anti-slavery town of Lawrence, which resulted in a four-hour orgy of blood and flames that left 150 dead and the town in smoldering ruins. Quantrill's force was more of a gang than an organized military unit – an embarrassment to the Confederacy – and represented an element of lawlessness and vendetta rampant in Kansas and Missouri that did not stop with the end of the war. Veterans of this border violence would write a new chapter in American history – with names like Jesse and Frank James, the Younger brothers, and other outlaws of the Wild West who once rode with Quantrill and his more evil protege "Bloody Bill" Anderson.

Things remained surprisingly quiet in Tennessee after the Battle of Stones River (or Murfreesboro), which had concluded January 2, and left the Union in possession of the battlefield. As Grant plotted the fall of Vicksburg and the Army of the Potomac fought one major battle and was on the verge of another in the East, General Rosecrans sat with his army at Murfreesboro, stockpiling, fortifying, and raising fears in Washington that Lincoln might have another McClellan on his hands. Bragg's Army of Tennessee was concentrated in and around Tullahoma, Tennessee, less than 40 miles away, and it was feared in Washington that Bragg might send reinforcements to Vicksburg unless he were otherwise occupied. After no small amount of prodding, Rosecrans prepared to move against Bragg. The Tullahoma Campaign of June 23-July 3 was extremely well executed by the Union commander, incurring few casualties as he outmaneuvered Bragg at every step, forcing the Confederates over the Tennessee River into Chattanooga, near the Georgia border. Rosecrans stopped pursuit and waited a month and a half before attempting to wrestle Bragg out of his new position.

Again after some prodding by Washington, Rosecrans planned a new offensive that would take his army across the Tennessee River south and west of Chattanooga and trap Bragg between his army and a force under General Burnside moving south from Kentucky into East Tennessee. Bragg

evacuated Chattanooga on September 6, and on that day Burnside occupied Knoxville. Maneuvering and blundering over the days to come culminated in the Battle of Chickamauga, September 19-20, fought along Chickamauga Creek in North Georgia. Reinforced by most of James Longstreet's corps of Lee's army, Bragg drove the Union army from the field in a tremendous tactical victory just when Southern spirits needed a lift. Rosecrans limped into Chattanooga, in the looming shadow of Lookout Mountain. The town proved to be a strong defensive position for Rosecrans, but he was now trapped there by the mountains, the Tennessee River, and Bragg's army. The Confederates occupied Lookout Mountain and Missionary Ridge and appeared immovable. Bragg laid siege and Rosecrans was stymied. A change in command was necessary.

General Grant arrived on October 23, as the new department commander, and General George H. Thomas – who'd given a good account himself in the late battle, earning the nickname "Rock of Chick-amauga" – succeeded Rose-crans as army commander. By the end of the month a "cracker line" was open, bringing ample supplies into the city. Reinforced with troops from other theaters which were now relatively quiet as winter approached, Grant soon launched a series of attacks to break out of Chattanooga.

On November 24, troops under General Joe Hooker – who like Burnside had stayed on in a subordinate role after failing as the Potomac army's commander – scaled Lookout Mountain and fought what has been called the Battle Above the Clouds, because of the dense fog clinging to the mountainsides. Next morning the Stars and Stripes fluttered conspicuously from high atop Lookout Mountain, providing inspiration to all the Yankees below. Later that day Union forces struck the Confederates on Missionary Ridge. Momentum on the Federals' part, not orders, and apprehension among the Confederates turned the attack into a foot race as charging Yankees swept startled Rebels completely from the ridge. Bragg's retreat did not stop until Dalton, Georgia, and all of Chattanooga and its mountains and ridges belonged to Grant. It would serve as a base for further operations into Georgia and the all-important Confederate supply center at Atlanta.

Joseph "Fighting Joe" Hooker replaced Burnside as the commander of the Army of the Potomac, but initially faired little better than his predecessor. His first real success came at Lookout Mountain on November 24, 1863.

The American Civil War was two and a half years old. There were green troops entering the ranks daily, to be sure, but they lined up next to battle-hardened veterans of countless engagements and long, weary marches. One price of war, as always, was the loss of innocence among the nation's youth. Young men not yet out of their teens had already experienced a lifetime's worth of fear, agony, and killing from too many battles, too many marches, too many glory-seeking officers, and too few comforts.

The whole complexion of warfare as the world knew it was changing. The days of saber-swinging cavaliers on horseback were over. More cavalrymen were killed by bullets while fighting dismounted than were knocked from the saddle by a saber slash. Stand-up fights between two well-disciplined armies drawn up close in an open meadow were of times past. Digging a trench might not seem the

near. In the North were Camps Douglas, Morton and Chase, Johnson's Island in Lake Erie, Elmira in New York, old Fort McHenry (of "Star Spangled Banner" fame) in Baltimore, Fort Delaware and others. The South had Libby Prison and Belle Isle, Florence and Salisbury in the Carolinas, Cahaba in Alabama and more, but the most notorious of all was the Confederate prison at Andersonville, Georgia, where in the summer of 1864 some 35,000 captive Union soldiers occupied living space of less than 25 acres, without barracks or adequate toilet facilities or sufficient food. Over 13,000 prisoners died at Andersonville, a hell-hole by any standards.

Feeding and supplying an army were constant logistics headaches: cut an army's supply line and it would have to retreat. That notion was tested in February and March as General William T. Sherman embarked on a campaign from Vicksburg across the State of Mississippi to Meridian on the Alabama

manly thing to do, but with the technical advances in weaponry, crouching in a ditch or behind a log helped keep you alive. By 1864 men's hearts and minds had grown cold, their actions machine-like on the march and in battle, and the glory of war no longer held as much fascination as in those early days back in '61. In short, they were better killers now. And a new concept of "total war" – making civilians as well as soldiers feel the sharp edge of Mars' sword – was put into play in 1864.

One instance of putting harsh necessity ahead of humanitarian instincts was the Union's decision to halt prisoner exchanges in order to exploit the South's manpower shortage. New prisons were built and old ones expanded in an attempt to accommodate the anticipated influx of prisoners, North and South, as the campaign season drew

border, generally destroying railroads and other resources in central Mississippi that the Confederacy might need. In the unusual, one-month, statewide march to Meridian and back, Sherman fought several skirmishes, took 400 prisoners, destroyed miles and miles of track, burned countless bales of cotton, commandeered 3,000 horses and mules, and all the while mostly lived off the enemy civilian population. It was a lesson that Sherman learned well and would try again on a larger scale.

Something else Sherman learned was that the South had a remarkable cavalry commander named Nathan Bedford Forrest, who fought from instinct rather than formal training, and whose simple philosophy was "War means fightin' and fightin' means killin'." In conjunction with Sherman's trek across Mississippi he was to have been assisted by

Sherman's famous (or infamous) "bummers" scoured the countryside for food, booty and contraband on the march through Georgia.

a cavalry force of 7,000 under General William Sooy Smith raiding south from Memphis. Smith never arrived. Hampered by the pesky Forrest, Smith tangled with him at West Point, Mississippi, on February 20, and he was soundly whipped by the Confederate "Wizard of the Saddle" on the 22nd at Okolona, one of Forrest's brightest moments. His most controversial fight was the capture of Fort Pillow above Memphis in April. Black garrison troops were allegedly massacred after they surrendered; the debate continues to this day. Forrest is considered by many to be the best horse soldier in American history. Sherman, who after the war said that "Forrest was the most remarkable man our Civil War produced on either side," at the time vowed to spend 10,000 lives and break the treasury if that's what it took to bring him down.

Meanwhile, U.S. Grant was promoted to the tone for the rest of the campaign as tough veterans fought desperately at close quarters and some were consumed in flames as the woods caught fire. The usual response to such a brutal and confused match as this was a hasty retrograde by the Army of the Potomac to refit and reorganize. But not with Grant supervising things. He plunged ahead, and the rank and file cheered him. They too were tired of defeat and humiliation.

Grant's Overland Campaign stalled for two weeks in May at Spotsylvania Court House as Lee's army constructed elaborate fieldworks and prepared to fight and die. Many did, and casualties mounted on both sides at a staggering rate as Grant vowed to fight it out on this line if it took all summer. The worst killing occurred in a 20-hour fight around a portion of the Confederate works that the men called the "Bloody Angle," a battle fought partially

revived grade of lieutenant general and placed in command of all Federal armies. He decided to locate his headquarters in the field, in the East with Meade's Army of the Potomac. Now the premier commander in the West would meet the premier commander in the East. Robert E. Lee of course had seen enemy generals come and go. The last one who had come from the West was John Pope. The last anyone had heard of him, he was way up in Minnesota fighting the Sioux.

The Army of the Potomac, under Grant's direction but still technically commanded by General Meade, left its winter camp around Culpeper, Virginia, and crossed the Rapidan River on May 4, entering a marshy, dense tangle of trees and underbrush known locally as the "Wilderness." Lee struck ferociously and this unlikely battlefield set the

during a driving rainstorm. Finally Lee pulled out and gave ground slowly as the Army of Northern Virginia fell back. The two armies battled constantly from Spotsylvania to the North Anna River, then Cold Harbor – where Grant was severely criticized for the appalling losses he suffered in a futile, ill-advised frontal attack on June 3 – then, by mid-June, to the James River and Petersburg, below Richmond, where the Confederates dug in for a do-or-die stand to protect their capital. Grant resorted to siege operations and he'd spend the next nine months confronting Lee on this line.

Considerable drama was provided along the siege lines on July 30, when the Federals exploded a mine under the Confederate works where the lines were very close together; Pennsylvania miners had dug the tunnel to the planned explosion site,

One of the most desparate engagements of the Civil War was the Battle of the Wilderness, where Grant opposed Lee directly for the first time. After two days of intense fighting, the losses on both sides were immense.

then it was packed with black powder and a fuse run to the mouth of the tunnel. The blast tossed humans, parts of fieldworks and huge chunks of earth into the air. The resulting attack, in which a number of black units participated, was horribly unsuccessful and Lee's troops quickly sealed the breach in their line. The whole affair entered the history books as the Battle of the Crater.

Grant's cavalry was under another commander brought from the West, General Philip Sheridan. Dispatched toward Richmond while Grant was stalled at Spotsylvania, Sheridan fought Stuart's cavalry at Yellow Tavern, north of the Confederate capital, on May 11 – a year and a day after Stonewall Jackson's death. Stuart was mortally wounded at Yellow Tavern and died in Richmond the next day. A month later Sheridan was defeated by Stuart's successor, General Wade Hampton of South Carolina, at Trevilian Station as the Union force raided railroads in Lee's rear.

In the West, where General Sherman assumed overall command with Grant's departure for the East, the invasion of Georgia was about to begin from the Federal base at Chattanooga. The key to the campaign was control of the railroads. Several of them criss-crossed at Atlanta, bringing in and shipping out supplies to points all over the South. One railroad, the Western & Atlantic, led south from Chattanooga to Atlanta. Along this route Sherman would advance. He had three armies under him: George Thomas' Army of the Cumberland, James B. McPherson's Army of the Tennessee, and John M. Schofield's tiny Army of the Ohio. All told, the three armies were still smaller than the Army of the Potomac, but larger than the Confederates' Army of Tennessee, still at Dalton. But Braxton Bragg had long since departed, resigning after the Missionary Ridge debacle to become President Davis' military advisor in Richmond. Bragg's replacement was Joe Johnston, who had made appearances in both major theaters of the war, was a capable commander, but who had never won, or lost, a significant battle (he outranked, but deferred command to General Beauregard at First Manassas, and was wounded at Seven Pines on the first day of that battle).

In a series of engagements through North Georgia, from Rocky Face Ridge to Resaca, then in and around Dallas, to the Kennesaw Mountain line, Sherman skillfully outmaneuvered Johnston by constantly thrusting at the Western & Atlantic Railroad, Johnston's supply link to Atlanta. President Davis and an anxious South watched through May and June as Johnston fell back from one defensive position to another, much the way he had done on the Peninsula facing McClellan back in '62. The president and the general had never seen eye to eye, but now they must reach an understanding. When or where would Johnston strike back at Sherman? Did Johnston have a plan to defeat Sherman? When Johnston evaded the question once too often, Davis relieved him, in mid-July, and appointed General John Bell Hood to command the army.

Hood was a known fighter, schooled as a tough division commander under Lee in Virginia. Hood sought to emulate the battle-winning exploits of his mentor and the great Stonewall Jackson. But his best laid plans for July attacks at Peachtree Creek, and along the Georgia Railroad east of the city (called the Battle of Atlanta), and at Ezra Church, outside the western defenses of Atlanta, all proved disastrous, and Sherman tightened his grip on the vital supply, rail and manufacturing center. A month more of skirmishing and maneuvering, and a hard-fought, two-day battle at Jonesboro (August 31-September 1) on the Macon & Western Railroad south of Atlanta, and the city fell. Mayor James Calhoun formally surrendered Atlanta to Sherman's men on September 2, but the Federals had failed to destroy the Confederate army. Hood's battered and bleeding command marched south to regroup.

While the first day's fighting raged at Jonesboro, in Chicago the Democrats nominated General George B. McClellan for president on the so-called "peace at any price" platform. Much of what transpired in Georgia over the next 48 hours led to McClellan's defeat in the November election, as a war-weary North could finally see victory in sight. Lincoln was re-elected for another term. Other contributing factors to Lincoln's victory at the polls were Admiral Farragut's victory ("damn the torpedoes") at Mobile Bay in August, and Phil Sheridan's successful campaign of destruction in the Shenandoah Valley. Back in Georgia during October, Hood had become restless and decided an offensive into Tennessee and perhaps Kentucky might erase Federal gains in the theater. He marched north from Palmetto, swung wide around Union-held Atlanta, crossed the Chattahoochee River, and tangled with Sherman's troops at Big Shanty, Acworth, Allatoona and Dalton, all north of Atlanta on the Western & Atlantic Railroad. Thus the armies had changed places from the opening of the Atlanta Campaign.

Sherman pursued Hood through North Georgia and into Alabama, then decided that whatever threat Hood posed could best be handled by troops gathering in Tennessee. He sent his trusted lieutenant George Thomas to Nashville to take command, and dispatched two corps under General John Schofield to assist in Tennessee. Sherman then abandoned his long and vulnerable supply line for a new base on the Atlantic coast. In mid-November he put the torch to Atlanta's warehouses, factories, railroad buildings and all other structures that might be used for war-making. Fires raged out of control and burned many private homes, churches, schools, the city hall, and other public and private buildings.

The "March to the Sea" across Georgia by

60,000 veterans, living off the land and the civilian population, and burning anything that could aid the Confederacy's war effort, ended with the capture of Savannah on December 21, which Sherman thought was a fitting Christmas gift for President Lincoln. Meanwhile, Hood's Tennessee Campaign met disaster at Franklin on November 30, after a missed opportunity at Spring Hill, below Franklin, allowed Schofield's two corps to get between Hood's army and Nashville. Any hope of Confederate success in Tennessee was dashed at the Battle of Nashville, December 15-16, where Thomas routed Hood's forces. But a remnant of Hood's army slipped away with a little fight left in it.

As the last winter of the war approached, the Confederacy had little hope of making up for the losses of 1864, in territory, strategic cities, and, most of all, in manpower. Lee had his back to

Crossroads in June; a July raid by General Jubal Early that took his Confederates to the edge of Washington's defenses and brought President Lincoln himself under fire while inspecting Fort Stevens on the defense perimeter; and Confederate cavalry commander John McCausland taking the war back into Pennsylvania and burning the town of Chambersburg.

But most of the news was bad for the South. In addition to setbacks already described, the famous Confederate raider *Alabama* was sunk by the *Kearsarge* off the coast of France; the raider *Florida* was captured off Brazil; and the ram *Albemarle* was sunk at its moorings in North Carolina. Confederate operatives in Canada launched several raids along the border and North Coast, with little success. A September raid on the Johnson's Island prisoner of war camp in Lake Erie ended in failure. The

Richmond, Atlanta was lost as a vital manufacturing and supply base. And west of the Mississippi, a last-ditch effort to take Missouri by Confederate General Sterling Price had failed. But, when all seemed lost to Southerners that year of 1864, there were incidents that had stirred the heart, such as the tiny Confederate submarine *Hunley* sinking the Federal sloop *Housatonic* near Charleston, South Carolina, in February; Virginia Military Institute cadets charging in a fight at New Market; yet another stunning victory for Forrest at Brice's

October raid on St. Albans, Vermont, was a dramatic affair as three banks were robbed and one citizen lay dead, but merely showed just how desperate the Confederacy was. The next month an attempt was made by Rebel agents to burn New York City, and this time a raider went to the gallows. Coincidentally, in New York performing in a production of *Julius Caesar* as the Confederates set fire to the building next door, was John Wilkes Booth, a young actor who passionately hated Lincoln. The two were on a collision course.

Soldiers of the 107th Colored Infantry, near Washington, D.C., late fall 1864. When black units fought in the front line, they acquitted themselves well, much to the surprise of their commanders.

As the new year dawned, the siege of Petersburg was over six months old. Rather than the quick marches and fluid maneuvers of the early war, the Civil War in the East had literally dug itself straight down into the earth. One dared not stick one's head above snow-capped trenchworks lest it be lost to sniper fire. Down the coast at Wilmington, North Carolina, the last major port still operable for the Confederacy, Federal land and naval forces pounded away at Fort Fisher. On Robert E. Lee's 58th birthday, January 19, Sherman's troops began leaving Savannah on what proved to be a most destructive, or "punitive," march up through South Carolina, the "mother of secession." By the end of the month, Lee was named General-in-Chief of all Confederate armies, hardly a desirable position considering the condition of things all over the Confederacy. "Marse Robert" remained with his beloved Army of Northern Virginia and did what he could to advise far-flung commands, hard-pressed at every point.

On February 3, a conference was held aboard the *River Queen* near Fortress Monroe, with Lincoln and Secretary of State William H. Seward attending on behalf of the United States, and Vice President Alexander H. Stephens the chief emissary for the South. What were the Confederacy's prospects and options for a negotiated peace? Lincoln held firm for the unconditional preservation of the Union, but implied liberal treatment of Southerners, a message repeated in his "With malice toward none" inaugural speech a month later.

February brought the fall of Wilmington, the evacuation of Charleston, and the capture of Columbia, South Carolina – the state capital – by Sherman's "bummers," the name his Westerners had acquired from foraging liberally off the land. The better part of Columbia was burned to the ground in a huge fire started by smoldering cotton bales left by retreating Confederates, then spread by high winds and arsonist Yankees of Sherman's command. The general himself claimed he never gave an order to burn the capital city, and if he had intended to burn it he would have done so and freely admitted it. In any event, tall, stark columns reaching to the sky from the ashes of Columbia's once elegant mansions and public buildings stood as monuments to the new era of warfare.

Sherman's troops entered North Carolina just after the first of March. Confronting him there were troops assembled under his old foe Joe Johnston. There would be some fighting and dying yet to come at Kinston, Fayetteville, Averasboro and Bentonville, but the war in this part of the country was all but over.

On March 13, President Davis signed into law a bill authorizing the recruitment of black troops to fight in Confederate service in exchange for their freedom. A year ago, before the fall of Atlanta and Wilmington, and before the siege lines had ringed Petersburg, when black units might have helped the Confederacy, General Patrick R. Cleburne proposed the recruitment of blacks and was severely denounced. He might have been drummed out of the army had he not been one of the best commanders the South had. Cleburne possibly was denied corps command because of his controversial idea, but now it was law, and Cleburne had died a division commander at Franklin the previous November.

The beginning of the end for the proud Confederacy began with rustling in the Army of the Potomac's camps in the last days of March. Lee's lines were stretched to breaking point at Petersburg, and break they did at the critical road junction of Five Forks when attacked on April 1. This action on Lee's extreme right flank exposed the South Side Railroad – a principal artery of supply and retreat – to Grant's grasp. Bad news reached President

Davis as he prayed at St. Paul's Episcopal Church in Richmond on Sunday morning, April 2: Richmond and Petersburg must be given up, and Lee was trying to extricate his army safely and get it moving westward. Many miles away, in Selma, Alabama, Nathan Bedford Forrest's command was beaten this same day. The last days of the Confederacy had arrived.

Everything of military value in Richmond was put to the torch by retreating Confederates. Grant's hordes marched through Petersburg and Richmond in pursuit of Lee's army on April 3. Even President Lincoln visited the conquered Rebel capital. As Davis fled south, Lincoln sat in his chair in Richmond. He, more than anyone, knew the trials and tribulations Davis had faced in this office.

Meanwhile, Lee's army struggled westward in

Jefferson Davis, a native of Kentucky, former soldier, Cabinet officer, Congressman and U.S. Senator from Mississippi, was the first and only President of the Confederate States of America.

need of supplies. He expected to find them at Amelia Court House, but they weren't there. His army was deserting him, melting away into the woods, while the remnant still intact sought crossings of the Appomattox River. Then even worse news arrived, if that were possible – a substantial part of the army was cut off and captured at the Battle of Sayler's Creek on April 6. Three days later it was all over. Lee surrendered to Grant at Appomattox Court House, Virginia, on April 9, 1865. This effectively ended the Civil War, for the remaining armies of the South soon followed suit, most notably Johnston's Army of Tennessee, which surrendered to Sherman on April 26, near Durham Station, North Carolina. The last land battle of the war occurred thousands of miles away near Brownsville, Texas, on May 12 – two days after Jefferson Davis was captured on the run in

The president died the next morning, uttering not a word on his deathbed. A cohort of Booth nearly killed Secretary of State Seward in a brutal attack at the same time Booth struck, but the planned assassination of Vice President Andrew Johnson had little chance of success, due to an unwilling assassin, who nevertheless went to the gallows. Three other co-conspirators were hanged, including Mary Surratt, the first woman executed by the Federal government. Several other accomplices, unwitting or otherwise, received prison terms. Booth was trapped in the Garrett family's tobacco barn in Virginia on April 26, and shot by a cavalry sergeant who perhaps miscalculated Booth's reactions when the barn was set afire to flush him out. Booth died a short time later.

A cruel fate had one black card yet to play. As Booth breathed his last on the Garrett's porch in

Georgia – and resulted in an inconsequential yet fairly won Confederate victory.

Two tragedies remained, even though the wholesale slaughter of Americans by Americans on the battlefield ended at the peace table in Wilmer McLean's parlor at Appomattox. On the evening of April 14, the same day the Stars and Stripes were run up Fort Sumter's flagpole after four long years, the actor John Wilkes Booth, embittered by the Union victory and emboldened by the fact that his family, mostly actors, had come to immortalize assassins – Shakespeare's plays supplied plenty of assassin-heroes – shot President Lincoln at Ford's Theatre.

Virginia, a steamer loaded with returning prisoners of war from the Confederate prison camps at Andersonville and Cahaba was churning its way up the Mississippi River. Later that night, seven miles above Memphis, the *Sultana's* boilers exploded, killing upwards of 1,800 people, the worst maritime disaster in American history. The *Sultana* was overloaded by many times its legal carrying capacity, probably because greedy Union officers in charge of shipping the prisoners home were receiving bribes from certain steamboat owners. Thus, the Grim Reaper gathered a final harvest of death even as peace and calm settled over a nation reunited.

The end of the Confederate dream came on April 9, 1865, when Lee met Grant to discuss the terms of surrender for the Army of Northern Virginia, in the parlor of the McLean home, near Appomattox Courthouse.

AFTERMATH

Reconstruction. That was the word used to describe how Southerners and their states were to be reassimilated into the American mainstream. Lincoln's plan, well thought out before his death and publicly announced or implied on numerous occasions, was a liberal policy of amnesty, based on the idea that the Southern states had never legally left the Union because the Constitution forbade it. It was believed that certain radical politicians had caused the secession trouble, and once clearer heads were in power the Southern states could resume roles in government. No punitive measures were ever a part of Lincoln's plan. This did not appeal to his Radical Republican contemporaries, who sought to punish the South and bar ex-Confederates from involvement in government at any level.

President Andrew Johnson – an irony of the sectional conflict just ended, being a North Carolinian by birth who called Tennessee home – carried out Lincoln's plan much the way the martyred president would have done, except that Johnson lacked the political skills Lincoln possessed. He clashed with the Radicals and narrowly escaped removal from office in impeachment proceedings in 1868. Such conflict led to more turmoil as occupation troops nested in the South with no end in sight. "Carpetbaggers" – Northern opportunists – picked at the Southern economy like vultures, often aided by Southerners who earned the name "Scalawags." Reconstruction, rather than being remembered as a period of reunion and rebuilding, came to be called the "Tragic Era" in the South.

But wounds began to heal. Jefferson Davis was released from prison in 1867, and Rebel generals such as Lee, Johnston and Forrest never saw a prison, let alone a noose, the usual price of unsuccessful civil uprising. Only Captain Henry Wirz, commandant of the Andersonville prison camp, was hanged for war crimes. The first state to secede, South Carolina, was readmitted to the Union June 25, 1868, but military occupation of the South remained until 1877, when home rule was restored during the administration of President Rutherford B. Hayes, a former Union general. This act has come to signify the end of Reconstruction – the final chapter of the American Civil War.

According to the 1860 census, there were four million slaves in America and almost a half-million free Negroes. In 1865, ex-slaves had little concept of their new-found freedom. Some still clung to their former owners, knowing no other life but servitude. Others took advantage of their freedom and embarked on their own pursuits of the American Dream. The 13th Amendment to the Constitution, enacted in 1865, ended slavery once and for all.

The 14th Amendment in 1868 granted citizenship, due process and equal protection under the law to blacks, followed in 1870 by the 15th Amendment which granted them the right to vote. The sudden enfranchisement of the Negro forced radical adjustments on the South, and it would take some time for matters to settle. Resistance to such change as well as the whole concept of Reconstruction and all the political, economic and social baggage it carried, gave rise to secret societies like the Ku Klux Klan, whose tactics ran the gamut from merely scaring blacks away from the polls to outright lynchings.

As the nation looked back on the tragic period of the 1860s one aspect stood out starkly against the light of reason – the dead, the many men and boys who died wearing Union blue or Confederate gray. Not until Vietnam was added in did American losses in all other wars finally surpass the loss of Americans in the Civil War, or the War Between the States, as Southerners preferred to call it. An estimated 600,000 deaths occurred in the war, with another 500,000 wounded who survived; the majority of deaths were from disease. Diarrhea and dysentery, typhoid fever, smallpox, measles and pneumonia were the leading killers, while drunken battlefield surgeons with filthy equipment claimed their share of deaths. Many horrible disfigurements and deaths resulted from amputations, the prescribed treatment for most battlefield wounds, but many miracles were performed and would-be mortalities lived to become old veterans, marching down Main Street, USA, on patriotic holidays, sometimes arm in arm with their former enemies.

The enduring legacy of the men in blue and gray is the commitment to principle they made, that hurled names such as Manassas, Shiloh, Jackson and Lee, Sherman and Grant, Gettysburg, Chickamauga, and Appomattox into international prominence. Except for the color of their uniform, these men were more alike than different, speaking the same language, worshipping the same God, and interpreting the same document of constitution.

At Appomattox, after the question of the Union had been settled by force of arms, a Southern soldier pointed to the Stars and Stripes and proclaimed that he would fight just as hard to protect and defend that banner as anyone present, regardless of uniform. And it is on this sort of positive note that Americans can draw hope and inspiration from what was truly the saddest and most tragic episode in American history, when brother fought brother. A new nation emerged, forged in battle and baptized in the blood of her youth – a new nation, indivisible, with liberty and justice for all.

Above: One of the great orators and statesmen of the pre-Civil War period was Daniel Webster (1782-1852), a New Englander who went to great lengths to prevent disunion in the country. He did not favor the institution of slavery in America, but felt that the possibility of a dissolution of the Union was a far greater evil than human bondage. Many credit Webster with postponing the war for a decade. A poll of U.S. senators in the mid-20th century resulted in Webster being named one of the top five "most useful" members ever to serve in the Senate.

Overleaf left: Boston-born and Harvard educated, Charles Sumner (1811-1874) never cared whom he offended and always seemed at the center of controversy. He railed against slavery, opposed the annexation of Texas and did not support the war with Mexico in the late 1840s. In the Congressional session of 1855-56, Sumner's anti-slavery views were cast upon the Senate's ears in a spleen-venting oration entitled "The Crime Against Kansas." It thrilled his extremist compatriots, but offended Southerners, and even led moderates to agree that the speech was "un-American and unpatriotic."

Overleaf right: The American Civil War has been called the world's first modern war. Steam locomotives had been first put to work in a military capacity to a minor extent during the Crimean War, but not until the Civil War in the United States were the railroads used extensively, making this war the first truly industrialized one in history. Trains played a critical role in the war and some campaigns were literally dictated by the slender fingers of a rail network. These "iron horses" could transport troops and supplies in a manner never before envisioned by military strategists. Pictured here is the first train to cross the Allegheny Mountains.

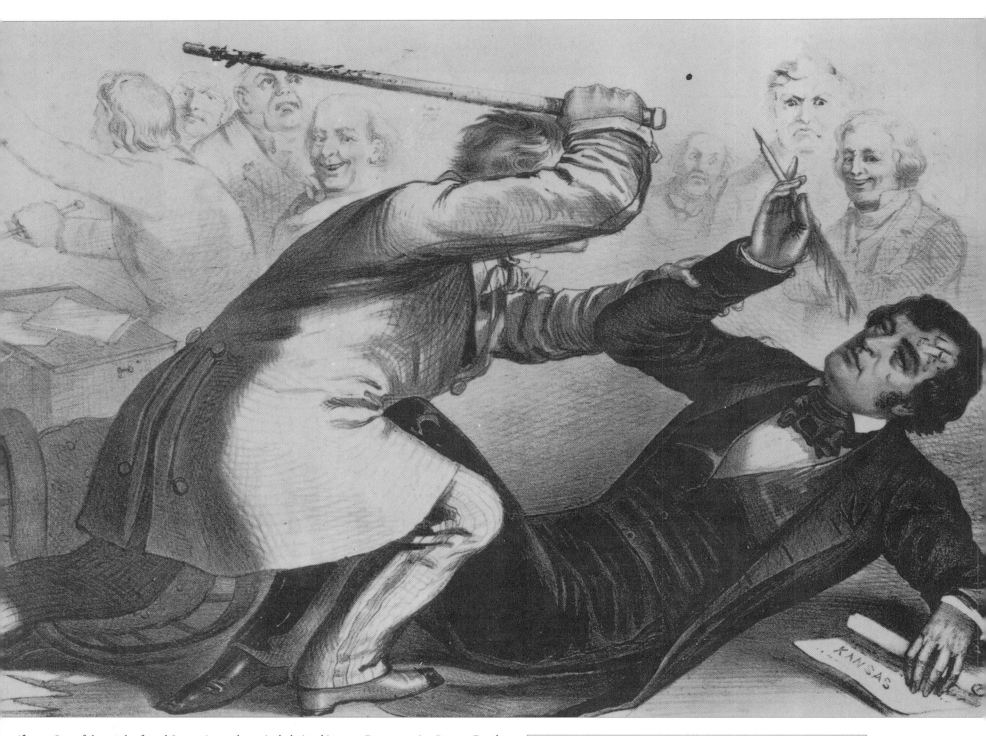

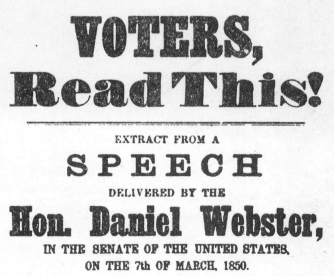

Above: One of those who found Sumner's words particularly insulting was Representative Preston Brooks of South Carolina. The Massachusetts senator had characterized slavery as a "mistress" and a "harlot," embraced by men like Senator Andrew Pickens Butler, one of Brooks' South Carolina colleagues and, worse, one of his kinsmen. Two days after the speech, Brooks walked into Senate chambers and cracked Sumner over the head with a sturdy cane, inflicting injuries from which Sumner never fully recovered. The abolitionist press made the most of the situation.

Right: Among Webster's greatest orations was the one delivered before the Senate in early 1850, which came to be referred to simply as his "Seventh of March Speech." Speaking "not as a Massachusetts man, nor as a Northern man, but as an American," his speech was in support of Henry Clay's compromise proposals. The thrust of the speech was "to beat down the Northern and Southern follies, now raging in equal extremes." He died in 1852, never knowing just how prophetic his words were – as the "infernal Fanatics" moved ever closer to deluging the country in blood.

Opposite: As educated, highly respected elected officials lashed out at one another with biting words or flailing canes, moving the nation ever closer to a violent showdown, perhaps the man missed most of all was the great Kentucky statesman, Henry Clay (1777-1852). He possessed keen insight and was by nature a conservative. Like Webster, more than anything else Clay wanted the Union preserved, and he was instrumental in the enactment of the Compromise of 1850. He died in 1852, after freeing his slaves. It was said of Clay that he did not possess the intellect of Webster, nor the philosophical powers of South Carolinian John C. Calhoun (1782-1850) – another political contemporary from the days of compromise – but for common sense and a grasp of human nature, Clay had no peer.

Opposite: Whole families of slaves were put to work picking and ginning cotton. The smallest ones of course were too young to work and were called "pickaninnies" – because they weren't "pickin' any" cotton. Twenty-five percent of the free white population of the South owned slaves, and it's a fact that some free blacks had slaveholdings. The heavy concentration of holdings was in the Deep South, the cotton states. In the Upper South and the Border States of Missouri, Kentucky and Maryland, slavery was not as prevalent. The institution of slavery in America thrived not because of a lack of civility on the part of Southerners, but rather because it was legal, and where it could make money it could make lots of money. Pictured here is a plantation near Savannah, Georgia.

Above: The banner proudly boasts 9,226 bales of cotton aboard the Mississippi steamer *Henry Frank*, evidence that "King Cotton" did in fact rule the South. Cotton dollars changed the Southern economy drastically during the first half of the nineteenth century, altering the South's position in the international trade arena from one of isolation and protection to an open-arms, free trade attitude. Thus, in the lifetime of the great South Carolina statesman John C. Calhoun, he went through the transformation from a defender of protective tariffs in 1816, to calling them "abominations" by 1828, "calculated to corrupt public virtue and destroy the liberty of the country." Export of cotton reached an all-time high.

Left: Cotton was "King" in the South. Eli Whitney's cotton gin revolutionized the industry, allowing one person to clean about 50 pounds of cotton each day. Born in Massachusetts in 1765, Whitney grew up under the tutelage of a father skilled in metal-working. The boy traded in his mechanical skills for book-learning and attended Yale. It was while he was studying law in Georgia in 1792 that Whitney first observed the extremely inefficient method used to extract seed from cotton. Falling back on skills early learned, he devised the cotton gin in 1793. Whitney is also credited with pioneering the use of interchangeable parts.

Above: William Lloyd Garrison (1805-1879) at age 22 became co-editor and publisher of the *National Philanthropist,* a paper outspoken against drinking and gambling. As early as 1829 he was getting in trouble by speaking out against slavery. He spent some time in jail in Baltimore for his writings, so in 1831 moved to safer abolitionist territory, Boston, and published the *Liberator* for the next 35 years. His abolitionist preachings once prompted the Georgia legislature to offer a $5,000 reward for his arrest. He publicly burned a copy of the U.S. Constitution because it sanctioned slavery.

Opposite: John Brown (1800-1859), shown here in an early portrait, was equally as outspoken against slavery as editorialist William Lloyd Garrison, but Brown sought to disprove the notion that the pen is mightier than the sword. Born in Connecticut to a father with abolitionist sympathies, Brown became a minister, then dabbled in several failed business ventures in Ohio. His strong feelings against slavery soon merged with the fire and brimstone of his religion to yield what Brown perceived to be a Divine mission, a crusade for freedom, an obsession that his powers of oratory imparted to his large family and other followers. He set out to destroy slavery by armed uprising.

Opposite: The alarm over Brown's raid on Harpers Ferry did not take long to reach Washington, 50 miles away. Dispatched to the scene with a small force of United States Marines was the fatherly-looking gentleman pictured here, Robert E. Lee, taken several years before the incident. Tagging along as Colonel Lee's volunteer aide-de-camp was young Lieutenant James Ewell Brown "Jeb" Stuart. In a short time Lee had matters under control. Brown was put under arrest and taken to nearby Charles Town for trial.

Below: The Kansas-Nebraska Act, which allowed the territories of Kansas and Nebraska to enter the Union as free or slave states based on a vote of the people, provided John Brown with just the right proving ground for his crusade. While there were not many outright abolitionists in this region, there were indeed plenty of "free-staters," people who did not want slavery in Kansas. In 1856 "Bleeding Kansas" became all the more sanguinary as Brown led the massacre of five pro-slavery men in retaliation for the murder of five free-staters. Three years later he planned his greatest adventure, the seizure of the Federal arsenal at Harpers Ferry, Virginia (now West Virginia), pictured here. His attack occurred on October 16, 1859, with a force of fewer than two dozen men, including several blacks. Though the intent was to arm local slaves with weapons from the arsenal and foment an uprising that would bring the institution of slavery crashing down across the South, within a few hours of the raid Brown found himself holed up in the engine house – soon known as "John Brown's Fort," the building closest on the left – with a few followers and some hostages.

Left: It mattered little that John Brown's uprising had been perpetrated against Federal property. He was in Virginia, in the custody of Virginians, and he was tried by a Virginia court. Here the white-bearded, charismatic old man gets his day in court. The cot at right evidences Brown's ailing health. He was seldom on his feet during the trial. The nature of the uprising gained full national attention, and the guilty verdict with death sentence provided the abolitionists with a martyr. The sketch is by James E. Taylor, noted artist of the Shenandoah Valley.

Above: Many a young man has become a soldier after hearing a patriotic speech or a rousing quick-step. Published in 1861, the words and tune of "John Brown's Body" brought many men and boys from the fields and shops into the ranks of the United States military. Even if you weren't an abolitionist, the thought of hanging Jeff Davis, or those "three rousing cheers for the Union," might be enough to captivate young men eager for adventure and glory.

Right: The climate of the states of the Deep South was ideal for cotton production, and Mr. Whitney's invention intensified the use of slave labor. Cotton came to be the mainstay of the Southern economy as production swelled to meet demand in Europe, particularly England, where textile manufacturing was a booming industry. By 1860 the South was producing over five million 400-pound bales annually. While Europeans might look with contempt upon America's "peculiar institution," slave labor, from a purely economical viewpoint, did indeed keep cotton prices down, and many people on both sides of the Atlantic, as well as both sides of the Mason-Dixon Line, prospered in the cotton trade.

Overleaf: Of similar importance to the war effort, North and South, was the steamboat, first put to significant use in a military capacity during the Mexican War. This notice from 1856 is an announcement for the *General Pike*, a passenger and mail packet. The boat is named for General Zebulon Pike (1779-1813), who explored the headwaters of the Mississippi River in 1805 and discovered the famous peak in Colorado named for him. Big river steamers generally had a useful life of less than ten years, and the same name might be carried forward to a new vessel as the old one was retired or destroyed. The steamer trade remained a lucrative business throughout the war, and in some instances became the source of greed and criminal conspiracy that cost soldiers' lives.

REGULAR PASS

THE NEW, ELEGANT AND FA

GENERA

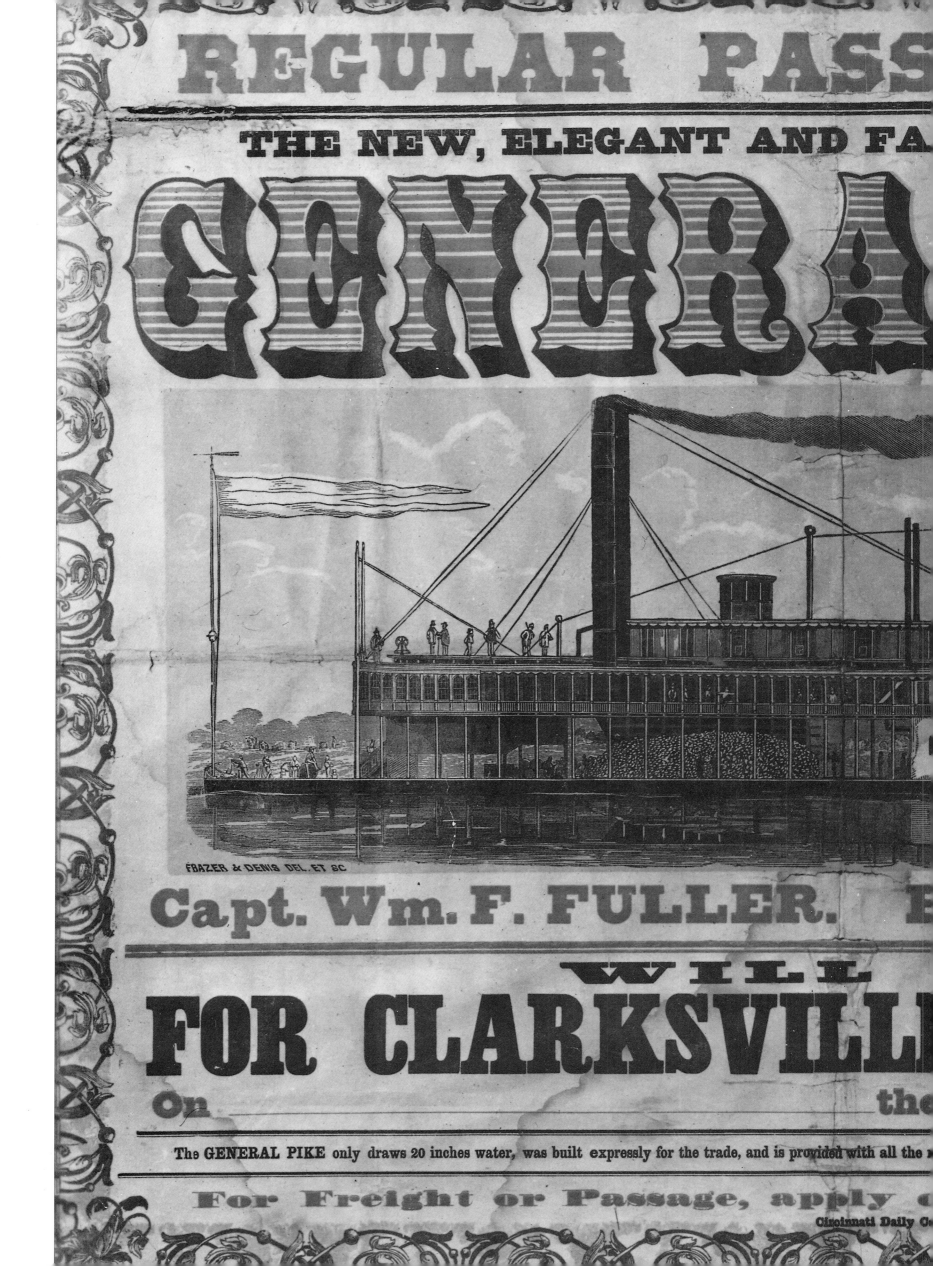

FRAZER & DENIS DEL. ET SC

Capt. Wm. F. FULLER.

WILL

FOR CLARKSVILL

On   the

The GENERAL PIKE only draws 20 inches water, was built expressly for the trade, and is provided with all the

For Freight or Passage, apply

Cincinnati Daily C

B-4157

SOUTH CAROLINA'S "ULTIMATUM".

Opposite: This photo of President James Buchanan (1791-1868) was taken by Mathew Brady, the well-known New York photographer whose fame would grow with his studio's images of Civil War battlefields – the first to be extensively documented by the camera. Buchanan was elected the 15th president in 1856 as the compromise candidate. Pennsylvania-born, Buchanan's stance was that, although he did not agree with slavery, he thought it was beyond the boundaries of the Federal government to interfere with the institution. Thus, support from Southern states helped put him in the White House during a period of growing unrest.

Above: This political cartoon portrays President Buchanan hoping to avoid war as his term draws to a close. South Carolina Governor Francis Pickens is poised to touch off war with a U.S.-made gun, as the president stands with his back to Fort Sumter, where the Stars and Stripes still flutter in peace. The days could not pass quickly enough for Buchanan. Other symbolism in the New York-published cartoon is the gun of war, named "Peace Maker." It is in position to send the governor to oblivion in his "ultimatum."

A NATION DIVIDED

Opposite: Born in a log cabin in backwoods Kentucky on February 12, 1809, Abraham Lincoln would come to embody the American Dream that anyone might rise above adversity and the humblest of beginnings to become President of the United States. He learned more of human nature and right and wrong around the cracker barrel and in real-life experiences clerking in a store, or in outdoor manual jobs, such as his inevitable depiction as a rail splitter, than many of his contemporaries learned from years of formal, expensive education. Some might call it common sense. Lincoln was one of the shrewdest politicians of all time.

Above: Stephen A. Douglas (1813-1861) was born in Vermont but relocated to Illinois, where he was instrumental in the founding of the Democratic party. His debates with Abraham Lincoln in 1858 received widespread notoriety. Not only were the two men political rivals, but social rivals as well, each having designs on one Mary Todd of Kentucky. The five-foot-four, 90 pound "Little Giant" lost to Lincoln in love and politics, but pledged support to his old adversary once Lincoln was elected president.

Above: This is the interior of Secession Hall in Charleston, South Carolina, where delegates decided that the best interests of their state were not being served by the election of the Republican candidate, Lincoln, in the November 1860 presidential election. Carolinians viewed the victory for the Republicans as a victory for abolition and Northern financial interests. The secession convention had at first convened in the state capital of Columbia, but adjourned to Charleston due to an outbreak of smallpox.

Opposite: This broadside announces the secession of the State of South Carolina. Known as the Palmetto State, South Carolina was the eighth of the original 13 colonies to ratify the Constitution, entering the Union on May 23, 1788, and the first state to leave the fold, declaring its bonds with the Union dissolved on December 20, 1860.

Overleaf: It was a joyous time in the streets of Charleston when secession was announced. The vote had been unanimous, 169 to 0, and such a powerful mandate was reflected in the mood of the people as torchlights and fireworks illuminated the city. Bands played throughout the night and military companies paraded in the streets. Nobody slept. Church bells rang out the glad tidings and orators took the podium to stir the excited populace to even greater heights of enthusiasm. Charleston was not alone in its celebration of independence, realized or hoped for. Fully a month earlier a similar demonstration occurred in Savannah, Georgia, depicted in this lithograph. Clearly the year 1860 ended on a note of celebration in the Deep South. In the North, the year was allowed to slip away with far less ceremony and joyfulness.

An Ordinance,

To dissolve the Union between the State of South Carolina and other States united with her under the compact entitled, "The Constitution of the United States of America."

We, the People of the State of South Carolina, in Convention assembled, do declare and ordain, and it is hereby declared and ordained,

That the Ordinance adopted by us in Convention, on the twenty-third day of May, in the year of our Lord one thousand seven hundred and eighty-eight, whereby the Constitution of the United States of America was ratified, and also, all Acts and parts of Acts of the General Assembly of this State, ratifying amendments of the said Constitution, are hereby repealed; and that the union now subsisting between South Carolina and other States, under the name of "The United States of America," is hereby dissolved.

EVANS & COGSWELL, PRINTERS, CHARLESTON.

Opposite: Jefferson Davis was born on June 3, 1808, in what is now Todd County, Kentucky, not many miles from the birthplace of Abraham Lincoln. While Lincoln drifted north with his family and eventually settled in Illinois, Davis' parents migrated southward to Mississippi. After a mediocre record at West Point, Davis put in his time at remote military posts and in 1835 married the daughter of Colonel (later General and President) Zachary Taylor. The marriage was only a few months old when his wife died of malaria. Over the next decade Davis prospered as a planter in Mississippi and in 1845 married Varina Howell of Natchez. After conspicuous service in the Mexican War, Davis' political aspirations and war record took him to the Senate and to President Franklin Pierce's cabinet as Secretary of War. This experience, both military and political, clearly gave Jefferson Davis advantages over Abraham Lincoln as the two men assumed chief executive roles in the spring of 1861.

Below: The first capital of the Confederacy was at Montgomery, Alabama. In the state capitol building, on Monday, February 18, 1861, Jefferson Davis was inaugurated the 1st President of the Provisional Confederate States. Unlike the four-year term of the United States presidency, the Confederacy allowed a six-year term. Stubborn, somewhat arrogant, and obsessed with such a penchant for detail that he insisted on reviewing almost every official War Department document, Davis obviously had his faults. Another failing was his blind support of friends he had placed in high positions of authority. He also lacked an understanding of the greater strategic aims of the war, and was not generally in tune with the international situation. Davis offset many of his faults by a complete and utter devotion to the cause of Southern independence. He never enjoyed widespread admiration by his constituents.

Above: In this political cartoon, Uncle Sam watches from a doorway as Jeff Davis sneaks out of the national house taking its household goods with him. Portrayed as a thief in the night, the Confederate president has Fort Sumter strapped to his back.

Opposite: The Confederacy's early political "chieftains," in addition to Jefferson Davis: Vice President Alexander H. Stephens of Georgia; Judah P. Benjamin of Louisiana, Attorney General (1861), Secretary of War (1861-1862), Secretary of State (1862-1865), perhaps the most capable member of Davis' cabinet; Robert Barnwell Rhett, noted "Fire-eater" and the Father of Secession as the drafter of South Carolina's secession ordinance (and soon-to-be harsh critic of Davis); John B. Floyd of Virginia, former U.S. Secretary of War, who would prove a military incompetent for the South; William Lowndes Yancey, "Fire-eater" and aspirant to the Confederate presidency, whose bitterness would turn him into one of Davis' antagonists; Isham G. Harris, Tennessee war governor who took to the field as an aide-de-camp when his state was overtaken by Federals; Robert Toombs of Georgia, nominee for the Confederate presidency, short-timer as Secretary of State (1861), and later brigadier general; John Slidell and James M. Mason, both diplomats, involved in the Trent Affair – they were seized from the British steamer *Trent* by a U.S. warship, an international incident that brought the North to the brink of war with England; and Henry Wise, ex-Governor of Virginia and later an inept military commander whose passion for the Southern cause was unexcelled.

JUDAH P. BENJAMIN.

ALEXANDER H. STEPHENS.

HENRY A. WISE.

R. BARNWELL RHETT.

JEFFERSON DAVIS.

JAMES M. MASON.

JOHN B. FLOYD.

JOHN SLIDELL.

WILLIAM L. YANCEY.

ROBERT TOOMBS.

ISHAM G. HARRIS.

Engᵈ by J. C. Buttre.

New York

CONFEDERATE CHIEFTAINS.

Below: Not long after Davis' inauguration the capital of the Confederacy was relocated to Richmond, Virginia. There the state capitol building became a meeting place for Confederate legislators. Relocation of the seat of government from Alabama to Virginia has been a source of debate since May 1861. Its proximity to Washington (100 miles) and the front lines of war made Richmond seem an unwise choice, but Virginia was the most populous state in the South, with agricultural and industrial resources the Confederacy badly needed. The Davis administration had, justifiably, a constant worry over the capital's safety. Such preoccupation and the resulting strain consumed considerable time, energy, money and manpower – things the Confederacy had little to spare.

Above: Pictured is a clean-shaven Abraham Lincoln taken about the time of his election. The beard would come later, allegedly at the suggestion of a young girl. Lincoln was in his early 50s, though some might guess him to be younger. Four years of war (and perhaps the effects of ill health not understood at the time) would greatly alter his appearance, making him look much older than his years. Grave doubts existed over Lincoln's ability to lead the country during the period of crisis. Many older, more experienced politicians felt they could manipulate the Westerner and gain for themselves the power they craved. Indeed, Lincoln's perception of the crisis seemed quite naive at this time, as when he addressed the Ohio legislature on February 13, and stated that "there is nothing going wrong" – when seven states had already seceded from the Union!

Overleaf left: At about one o'clock on the afternoon of Monday, March 4, 1861, Lincoln appeared on a platform constructed on the portico of the Capitol to be inaugurated the 16th President. The Capitol dome was not yet completed. Crowds thronged to hear the new president give his address, and troops kept a watch for snipers who might appear at any moment in nearby windows. Just getting to Washington from Illinois had involved a certain amount of intrigue and danger. Rumors of assassination plots were rampant in Baltimore, a stop on the way to the capital city. The man who held Lincoln's hat as he addressed the crowd at the inauguration was his old Illinois rival, Senator Stephen Douglas. Though the nation might be divided, the State of Illinois stood as one.

Overleaf right: William H. Seward (1801-1872) was a New Yorker, a free-soil advocate, a Republican and a presidential hopeful – and one of those who thought he could usurp power from Lincoln and effectively assume the reins of government. Seward served as Secretary of State for the whole of the war. After some initial blunders, such as urging a war with Europe in order to reunite the states in a common cause, Seward calmed down and proved an able diplomat. His most controversial act was after the war when he negotiated the purchase of Alaska from Russia.

Opposite: Commander of the Union garrison at Fort Sumter was Robert Anderson (1805-1871). Born near Louisville, Kentucky, of a father who had served as an officer in the Revolutionary War, Anderson graduated from West Point in 1825. After service in the Black Hawk, Seminole and Mexican wars, he was elevated to the rank of major in 1857. In November 1860 Anderson was ordered to Charleston to take command of its harbor defenses, which included Forts Moultrie and Sumter. Being a pro-slavery man married to a Georgia lady, he might not have been the wisest choice. Soon after South Carolina's secession, Anderson abandoned Fort Moultrie as too vulnerable to attack from the mainland and moved his garrison of some 130 men to the yet uncompleted Fort Sumter – and an anxious nation watched and waited.

Below: Artist William Waud sketched this scene on Morris Island in Charleston Harbor, South Carolina. Under the direction of Confederate engineers, Negroes are being used to set guns in a hastily-built installation facing Fort Sumter. National attention had become focused on Fort Sumter, situated on a tiny, man-made island in the center of the harbor, since the previous December 26, several days after South Carolina had seceded and the day the Union garrison from Fort Moultrie moved to the better protection offered by the island fort. Demands by the state for the surrender of all Federal property within its borders had resulted in a stalemate of wills.

Previous pages: Subordinate commanders in Anderson's garrison included: (seated left to right) Captain Abner Doubleday, Major Anderson, Assistant Surgeon Samuel W. Crawford, and Captain John G. Foster; (standing left to right) Captain Truman Seymour, Lieutenant G.W. Snyder, Lieutenant Jefferson C. Davis (no relation to the Confederate president), and Lieutenant R.K. Meade. Before war's end, Doubleday would rise to brigadier general, but he is best remembered for his connection to the development (not invention) of the great American pastime, baseball. Crawford, Seymour and Davis also ended the war as brigadiers, and Foster a major general. Snyder died in 1861 and never realized his full potential. Meade served his post well, but after the fall of Fort Sumter the Virginia-born officer resigned his commission, and at the time of his death in 1862 he was a major in Confederate service.

Right: The problem of the Union passed from the political to the military arena at four-thirty on the morning of April 12, 1861, when the first Confederate shell burst over Fort Sumter. Soon the harbor was ringed with fire as other batteries joined the bombardment. Depicted here is the scene inside one of the Confederate installations as one of the guns is destroyed. In the distance is Fort Sumter, sitting alone in the middle of the harbor. Inside Fort Sumter, Major Anderson cautioned his men to waste none of their fire, as their supply of ammunition was limited. Captain Doubleday fired the first retaliatory shot of the United States at about seven that morning, when daylight offered better targets.

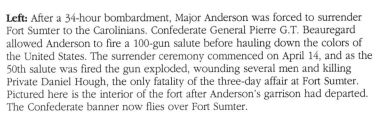

Left: After a 34-hour bombardment, Major Anderson was forced to surrender Fort Sumter to the Carolinians. Confederate General Pierre G.T. Beauregard allowed Anderson to fire a 100-gun salute before hauling down the colors of the United States. The surrender ceremony commenced on April 14, and as the 50th salute was fired the gun exploded, wounding several men and killing Private Daniel Hough, the only fatality of the three-day affair at Fort Sumter. Pictured here is the interior of the fort after Anderson's garrison had departed. The Confederate banner now flies over Fort Sumter.

Above: Reaction to Lincoln's call for volunteers was met with less enthusiasm in the Border and Upper South states. Kentucky and North Carolina responded with a firm "No." Indeed, North Carolinians marched into Fort Macon on the coast and claimed the unmanned Federal installation for themselves. In not too many days the states of Virginia, North Carolina, Tennessee and Arkansas seceded from the Union; Kentucky, Missouri, Maryland and Delaware were torn in their sentiments. The same patriotic spirit that gripped the North spread to the South for its opposition cause. Depicted here is a recruiting drive for the Confederate army in Woodstock, Virginia.

Opposite: On April 15, 1861, President Lincoln issued a proclamation that a state of insurrection existed, and he called for 75,000 men to put down the rebellion. Militiamen from states across the North answered the call immediately. From Maine to Minnesota, men and boys read inspired editorials and listened to patriotic songs and roaring political speeches. Lincoln had called out the troops! The days of waiting were over. Bugles sounded and drums beat out a rally cadence. Shops and factories and fields emptied. It was such an exciting time.

Overleaf left: The archive description of this photo reads: "A well equipped Confederate infantry private early in the war." An estimated six to seven million white Americans lived in seceded states, or were sympathetic to the Confederate cause but living in areas still largely adhering to the Union. The typical Southern soldier was a farmer in his late teens or early 20s, who worked the family farm without the use of slave labor, which was a luxury of the upper classes. There were fewer than 400,000 slaveholders in the South by the time the Civil War began.

Overleaf right: This young Confederate soldier, identified as Walter Miles Parker, appears more plainly attired and equipped than the previous soldier. He faced an uphill struggle from the outset. The North had three times the population (compared to Southern whites only) and a far superior industrial advantage. The typical Southerner fought not to save the institution of slavery for the upper classes. Perhaps the best reason for taking up arms against the North was given by a Southern boy to his Yankee captor: "Cause y'all are down here."

Above: Fort Sumter was not the only focus of attention in the spring of '61. Pictured here is another target of Southern hope, Fort Pickens at Pensacola, Florida. Pickens, along with two other installations, guarded the harbor and the Pensacola Navy Yard, considered the best in the Deep South. Commanding United States forces at Pensacola was Lieutenant Adam J. Slemmer. Several surrender demands were made and each time Slemmer refused. Similar to the situation at Sumter, a reinforcing vessel, the *Brooklyn*, was held at bay for a time, pending negotiations with Confederate and Florida officials. When Lincoln took office in March, he ordered the immediate supply and reinforcement of Fort Pickens, but bureaucratic red tape held up landings at the fort until after the Confederates had opened fire on Fort Sumter.

Opposite: With the outbreak of war, the Union garrison at Fort Pickens was reinforced by 200 men aboard the *Brooklyn*. In a short time a thousand more men were landed, and four warships were present to protect the fort and harbor. Some 5,000 Confederates under General Braxton Bragg commenced siege operations and prepared to invade Santa Rosa Island, upon which sat Fort Pickens. Pictured here are men of Bragg's command, in camp at Pensacola in 1861. They are from the 9th Mississippi Infantry, a unit that would see hard fighting before the war ended, at places like Chickamauga, Missionary Ridge, Atlanta.

Below: Involved in operations in Florida at this time was Company B, the "Independent Blues," of the 3rd Florida Infantry, whose flag is pictured. Unfortunately for the Confederates, Fort Pickens remained in Union hands the whole war. Further reinforced with men and naval support, the fort withstood several severe bombardments. Bragg's troops evacuated the town of Pensacola on May 9, and the Federals occupied it three days later.

Opposite: Within days of the fall of Fort Sumter, the 7th New York Infantry was mustered in and prepared to leave for the front. The unit, organized in New York City, is pictured here assembled on the Bowery near the Cooper Institute, also known as Cooper Union. The 7th's first duty was at Newport News, Virginia, and they participated in the Battle of Big Bethel on June 10, 1861, a small engagement that proved an embarrassment to the North and a boost to Southern spirits. The New Yorkers were in the Peninsula Campaign of 1862 and, except for Second Bull Run, all the major battles of the Army of the Potomac until May 1863, just after Chancellorsville, when they were mustered out.

Opposite top: Baltimore, Maryland was a city seething with secessionist sympathies. It was on the principal rail route connecting Washington with the West and Northeast. On April 19, 1861 a train carrying the 6th Massachusetts Infantry to Washington in response to Lincoln's call for volunteers was surrounded by an angry mob as the train entered town. In the ensuing riot, depicted here, the Massachusetts regiment lost four dead and 39 wounded. Baltimore's mayor reported 12 civilians killed, and dozens were wounded. For nearly a month chaos reigned, troops could not be brought through Baltimore, and Washington was effectively isolated. On May 13, Brigadier General Benjamin F. Butler marched to Baltimore with the 8th Massachusetts in a driving storm, seized high ground overlooking the city, fortified the position with artillery, and for the rest of the war Baltimore was under martial law.

Opposite bottom: The 26th New York Infantry, known as the "Second Oneida Regiment," was organized at Elmira, New York in May 1861, and left the state for duty in the defenses of Washington and at Fort Lyon, where this picture was taken. The unit later fought at Cedar Mountain, Second Bull Run, South Mountain, Antietam, Fredericksburg and Chancellorsville, before being mustered out in late May 1863. Battle losses were five officers and 101 men killed or mortally wounded in battle, and 42 men lost to disease.

Right: General Pierre Gustave Toutant Beauregard (1818-1893) was the Confederate hero of Fort Sumter. An 1838 graduate of West Point, second in his class of 45 students, Beauregard served in the Mexican War, during which he achieved a conspicuous record as an engineer under General Winfield Scott. Afterward Beauregard supervised the construction of coastal fortifications and from 1858-1861 was chief engineer at New Orleans. In January 1861 he was appointed superintendent of West Point, but was relieved after only a few days because of questions over his loyalty. Beauregard's home state of Louisiana left the Union on January 26. In February he resigned from the U.S. Army and cast his lot with the seceded states. After the successful siege of Fort Sumter, Beauregard was transferred to Virginia, where he participated in the first major land battle of the war.

Above: One of the great dramatic moments of the Battle of Bull Run was the charge of Colonel Michael Corcoran's 69th New York Militia on a Rebel battery. A native of Ireland, Corcoran had resigned from his job on the police force as a result of disagreement with British policy and went to the United States. In New York he held several jobs and became active in the militia, earning the rank of colonel by 1859. After refusing to call out his regiment to honor the visiting Prince of Wales, Corcoran was arrested and was facing court martial at the time of Fort Sumter. Charges were dropped so he could volunteer his services to the Union. At Bull Run he was wounded and captured while leading his 69th Militia and spent a year in a Confederate prison, where he became a pawn in the prisoner exchange game. The hard-bitten colonel was promoted to brigadier general to date from the Battle of Bull Run. He was killed in a fluke accident in December 1863, when his horse stumbled and fell.

Opposite: General Beauregard was in command of troops at Manassas Junction in northern Virginia when Union Brigadier General Irvin McDowell of Ohio, prodded into taking the field with his ill-trained army of recruits by public pressure and the approaching termination of many of his army's three-month enlistments, marched from Washington to give battle in what was expected to be the single decisive clash of the rebellion. Pictured here is the Stone House on the battlefield of Manassas, fought July 21, 1861 and called the Battle of Bull Run in the North. As the battle heightened, the Stone House found itself caught between opposing lines. It served as a hospital.

Overleaf: On the Confederate side – where the engagement was called the Battle of Manassas – one of the most dramatic moments was provided by that eccentric former professor at Virginia Military Institute who had witnessed John Brown's execution and at Manassas led a brigade of Virginians. The tide-turning factor in the Southern victory was the timely arrival of forces under General Joseph E. Johnston to reinforce Beauregard. Among those reinforcements was the brigade under the former professor, Thomas J. Jackson, pictured here. At a critical point in the battle, Jackson's men held their position on Henry House Hill and other commanders urged their men to rally around them, for Jackson's Virginians appeared to stand like a "stone wall" in the face of stiff opposition. Jackson earned the nickname "Stonewall" that day, and his exploits became legendary.

Confederate States of America,
WAR DEPARTMENT.

Richmond _Aug 31st 1861._

Sir:

You are hereby informed that the President has appointed you _by and with the advice and consent of Congress a_ **General** _to take rank June 14th 1861_

IN THE ARMY OF THE CONFEDERATE STATES. You are requested to signify your acceptance or non=acceptance of said appointment: and should you accept you will sign before a magistrate, the oath of office herewith, and forward the same with your letter of acceptance to this Department.

L P Walker
Secretary of War.

General Robert E Lee C.S.a.
Commanding &c
Staunton Va

Above: Another Confederate commander who at this time was largely an unknown quantity, except by reputation – he had refused the chief command of United States forces, offered by General Winfield Scott – was Robert E. Lee of Virginia, whose loyalty to his state was foremost. Lee was appointed a brigadier general in May 1861, the highest rank allowed by Confederate States law at the time. Then, on August 31, 1861, as set forth in the document reproduced here, Lee was elevated to the rank of full general, to date from the previous June 14. Signing the document was Alabamian Leroy Pope Walker, the Confederacy's first Secretary of War, who held the post until his resignation in September 1861.

Left: West of the Mississippi River a spirited battle took place along Wilson's Creek near Springfield, Missouri on August 10, 1861. While a Southern victory, the Unionists under Brigadier General Nathaniel Lyon (pictured) were outnumbered, and as the attackers inflicted severe casualties on the Confederate forces of Brigadier General Ben McCulloch, who were taken by surprise in the opening assault. The battle was described as "the hardest four hours' fighting that up to that time had ever taken place on the American continent." One of the dead from the battle was General Lyon. Born in Connecticut on July 14, 1818, Lyon was a West Point graduate and veteran of the Seminole and Mexican wars. In Missouri in 1861, Lyon was either loved or hated. His decisive if not harsh hand-ling of affairs in Missouri enraged Confederate adherents, and in loyalist circles earned for Lyon the reputation as the man who saved Missouri for the Union.

Above: "Fall In for Soup" is the title of this sketch by noted Civil War artist Edwin Forbes, who covered the war for *Frank Leslie's Illustrated Newspaper*. Notice the rows of tents and the chimneys fashioned from barrels, indicating this was not a temporary campsite. The area has been cleared, as evidenced by the many tree stumps. Some of the logs have been used to construct sturdy tent bases.

Opposite: For every day that a soldier spent in combat he spent many, many more in camp and on the march, where the "glory" of war became lost amid routine, boredom and loneliness.

B-245
20

Above: Pictured are typical utensils of a Civil War soldier, and the most common item of his diet, whether a Northern or Southern man: hardtack, or "army bread." The quarter-inch thick, square crackers of unleavened flour became the butt of many jokes. Some men laughingly noted that the only protein in their diet was the worms in their hardtack. Many questioned whether the stuff had been manufactured 15 years before, during the Mexican War. Indeed, it was considered to have an incredible shelf life. In the mid-1870s, troopers on the plains campaigning against Indians opened ration boxes dated 1863.

Right: Letters and packages from home were a link between the monotony of camp and horrors of battle and the tranquility of hearth and home. The Adams Express Company was one of the earliest package delivery firms, and the men shown here were undoubtedly popular figures around camp. Deliveries went both ways, though, and one of the less pleasurable tasks they performed was shipping home a soldier's effects following his death in the camp hospital.

Above: At remote outposts you made do with what you had. This camp of Confederates in Texas is being provisioned from army wagons clearly marked "U.S." and the quartermaster boxes carry the same letters. The sketch was made by a soldier named Iwansky and somehow turned up in a Northern publication in June 1861. The boys seem to be having a high time. Their benefactor, besides the Federal government, was Union General David E. Twiggs, who with Winfield Scott, John E. Wool and William S. Harney, comprised the entire roster of line generals as the Civil War approached. Twiggs was the only one of the four to go with the South. He was dismissed from United States service in March 1861, after surrendering everybody and everything under his command to secessionist Texans without so much as a fight or even a shot being fired. The 70-year-old Twiggs was appointed a major general in the Confederacy in May 1861, but he died from infirmities of age the following year. The Texan holding up a bottle at far left might well be toasting the old general.

Left: This photograph by the Mathew Brady firm shows the drill of a Union field gun crew. Each man has a role in serving the rifled piece, and the most important one at the moment is the fellow in full view on the right. He is holding the lanyard (a string) attached to a friction primer at the breech of the gun barrel. He yanks the lanyard, a spark is created that ignites the powder, and the gun fires. Practice makes perfect, and the time spent drilling in camp could make the difference between life and death for this crew.

Overleaf left: Another popular figure around camp was the newspaperman. The war correspondent, mind you, might not be as welcome, since many generals considered him a pest or even unwitting spy, who might reveal camp secrets and troop strengths in the course of his reporting. But the man who brought the papers always found willing customers in camp – even the general himself. Moreover, in both armies a number of officers and men served as informal correspondents, sending articles on camp life and battles to newspapers back home.

Overleaf right, top: This Alexander Gardner photo shows peddlers of Philadelphia, New York and Baltimore papers at their newsstand in the field. Much of the printed word that came straight from the battlefronts was inaccurate and generally exaggerated the hometown side. Nevertheless, the newspaper was the principal medium of mass communication for the times. Papers published in enemy cities were always in high demand and special agents risked their lives getting papers through the lines. One never knew what tidbit of information might be gleaned from the enemy's newspaper that would alter or launch a major movement or campaign. It was said that Jefferson Davis had New York papers on his desk even before the ink was dry.

Overleaf right, bottom: "War Songs" is the title of this pencil sketch by Winslow Homer of *Harper's Weekly.* His specialty was depicting the routine of life in camp with all its day-to-day frustrations, joys and humorous incidents. Singing was a favorite pastime in camp and after a particularly moving rendition of a song about home, grown warriors might have tears streaming down their cheeks. Equally arousing were the patriotic songs – the songs that made the clerk set aside his arm bands for a shell jacket, and the farmer trade his plow for a musket.

Above: Edwin Forbes sketched this camp scene of a musician and his "pard." There won't be any fighting or drilling for the moment, because the musket seems far from their thoughts. Those aren't Indians camped in the background at left. The conical shaped shelters were called "Sibley tents," named for their inventor, Henry Hopkins Sibley, who left Federal service at the outbreak of war and joined the Confederacy. Prior to the war the Sibley tent was in widespread use. It could accommodate up to 20 men and their gear, and even had room for a stove or fire pit in the center. The tent proved most useful for garrisons or long-term camps, but armies on the move soon found them cumbersome to haul around and adopted the "pup tent" or shelter-half instead.

Below: In many instances, especially during the winter, officers had their wives stay in camp with them. Captured here by the talents of artist Alfred R. Waud is the marriage ceremony of Captain Daniel Hart and Miss Ellen Lammond, performed by Chaplain Julius D. Rose in the camp of the 7th New Jersey Infantry on March 12, 1863. In attendance were all of the principal officers of the Third Corps, Army of the Potomac, including Major General Daniel E. Sickles, corps commander. Also attending as guest of honor was the new army commander, Major General Joseph Hooker. Alfred, the better known of the two Waud brothers (the other was William, also a sketchist), did not draw camp scenes only, but also armed himself and got close enough to the action to sketch battle scenes. The two Wauds produced hundreds of sketches of the Civil War and postwar South and West. This drawing appeared in the April 4, 1863 edition of *Harper's Weekly*. The Harts were natives of Philipsburg, New Jersey. The captain survived the war, but in 1878 died after suffering a bout of the malaria he had contracted during it. At the time of his death he was a major in command of Fort Stockton in Texas.

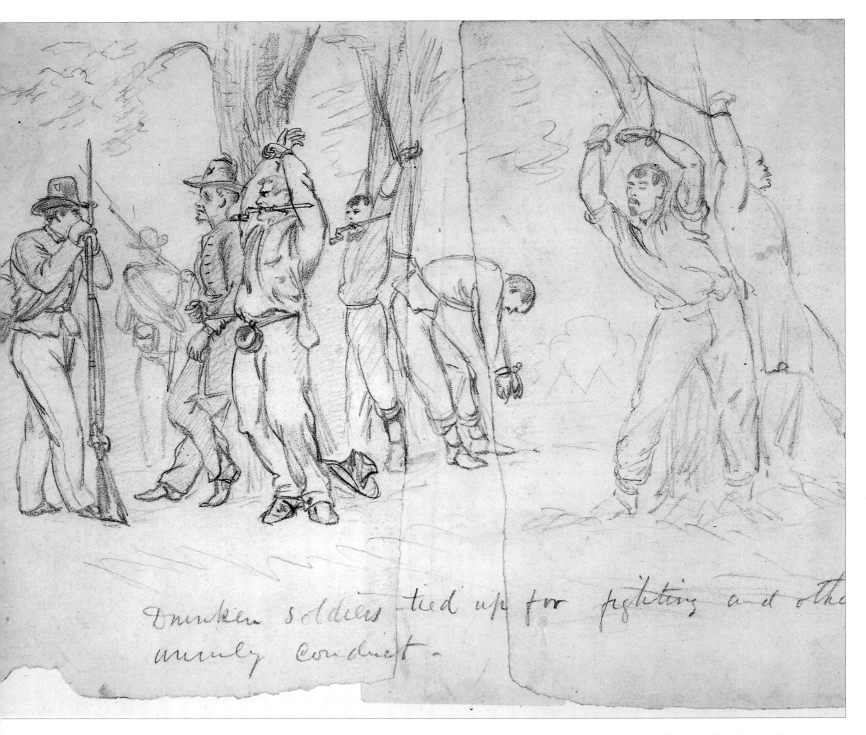

Drunken soldiers tied up for fighting and other unruly conduct.

Above: As with soldiers since the first army marched, their free time might be consumed in drinking and carousing and brawling. Civil War armies were no exception. It was not unusual for someone's canteen to be full of corn liquor or other spirits. When they got out of hand it was the provost marshal who rounded them up and placed them under arrest. The unfortunate fellows sketched here are suffering the penalty for drunken unruliness, though different camps might have different punishments. These men have all been tied up and two of them are gagged with bayonets. The one in the center looks exhausted; the man against the tree and facing the guard appears to have a blackened eye. Save it for the enemy, was the advice usually given.

Opposite top: When the army didn't adequately supply the needs of camp, soldiers might resort to "foraging." Generally this was not allowed and a soldier might face punishment for stealing from civilians. This fellow has rounded himself up an ox, and some cattle are being herded by others in the background. By the time the war was over the concept of foraging had taken on a new meaning. Entire armies abandoned their supply bases and proved that they could move faster when unencumbered with bulky trains and not dependent on tenuous links to some distant depot. Instead, they lived off the enemy civilian population. Early in the war, though, before foraging became the vogue, the most popular man in camp was the one who could steal a pig or chicken and treat his messmates to an unexpected and illegal feast.

Opposite bottom: This Edwin Forbes drawing depicts a lonely sentry preparing Christmas dinner at his post. The sentiment is universal. Loneliness was often the soldier's worst hardship. Even in the midst of tens of thousands of others, soldiers far from home and loved ones could be lonely, especially on such an occasion as Christmas. The American image of Santa Claus came from the Civil War, when artist Thomas Nast sketched a jolly old fellow with long white beard visiting an army camp and distributing gifts to the men. As the year 1861 drew to a close, the nation had been at war for less than nine months. Suffering and bloodshed would intensify over the coming years as the men became better trained soldiers, better killers. Three more Christmases came and went before peace spread across the land.

A Christmas dinner

Above: Some of the biggest news of 1862 involved this man, Major General George B. McClellan (1826-1885). As for military training and experience, "Little Mac" had few peers. Born in Philadelphia to a well-to-do family, he attended various preparatory schools and the University of Pennsylvania before entering West Point, from which he graduated second in his class of 59 men in 1846. As was the custom with top graduates, McClellan was posted to the Corps of Engineers. During the Mexican War he distinguished himself while serving under the direct eye of General Winfield Scott. Afterward McClellan was an instructor at West Point and eagerly translated from the French a manual on bayonet drill and adopted it to the army's instruction. Then the young officer embarked on a series of engineering duties and fact-finding expeditions. As one of a group of selected officers, McClellan was sent to Europe as an observer during the Crimean War. There he had the opportunity to examine the equipage of European troops, and upon his return to the States he developed the "McClellan saddle," which was adopted by the cavalry. In 1857 private business lured him away from the army to become chief engineer of the Illinois Central Railroad, and by the time of the Civil War he was living in Cincinnati as president of the Ohio & Mississippi Railroad. He was 34 years old.

Opposite: As is evidenced by the lines at the top of this recruiting poster, George McClellan gave up his well paid civilian profession to serve his country when the war broke out. Ten days after the fall of Fort Sumter he was appointed major general of Ohio troops, and three weeks later, based solely on reputation, President Lincoln made him a major general in the Regular Army, outranked only by 74-year-old General-in-Chief Winfield Scott. Commanding in western Virginia, McClellan had success in minor engagements, but it was more than other Federal commanders had been able to achieve in other theaters. After the defeat of McDowell's Union army at Bull Run, McClellan was given command of that shattered and demoralized force and rebuilt it, added to it – as per the recruiting poster – and called it the Army of the Potomac. When General Scott retired in late 1861, McClellan became the General-in-Chief of all the armies of the United States.

HEAVY ARTILLERY

Raised by authority of the State, at the request of the Secretary of War and Major-General McCLELLAN.

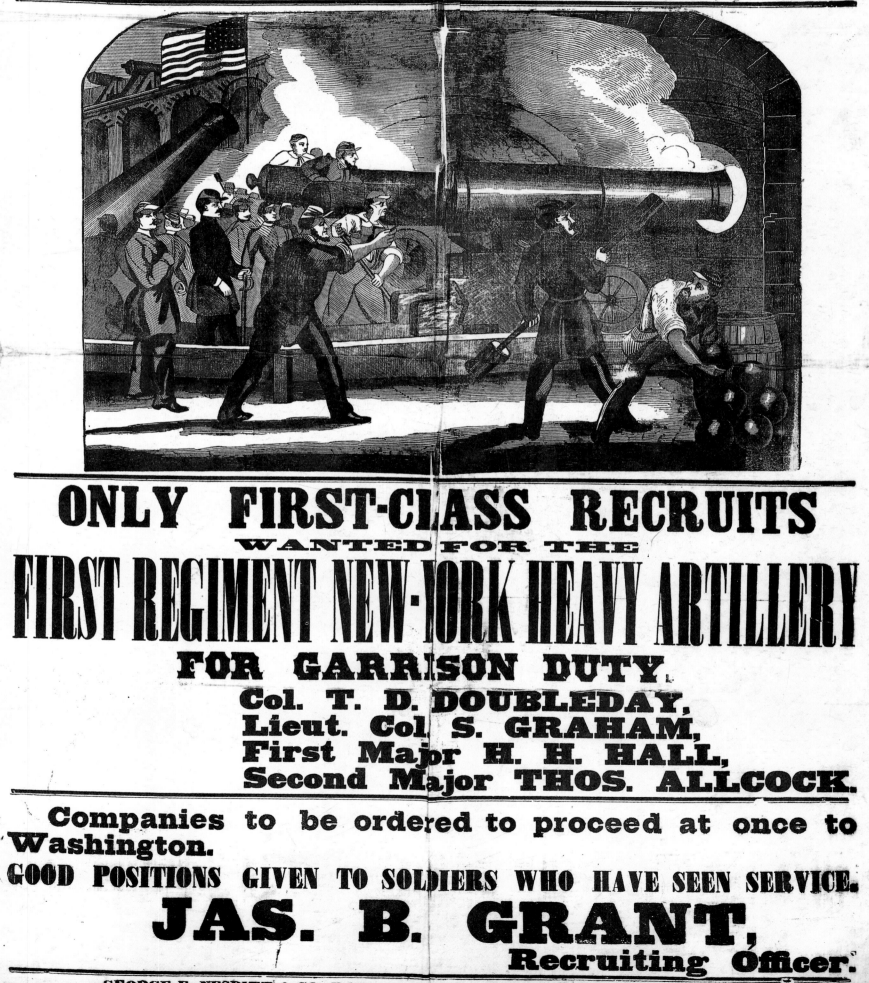

ONLY FIRST-CLASS RECRUITS
WANTED FOR THE
FIRST REGIMENT NEW-YORK HEAVY ARTILLERY
FOR GARRISON DUTY.

Col. T. D. DOUBLEDAY,
Lieut. Col. S. GRAHAM,
First Major H. H. HALL,
Second Major THOS. ALLCOCK.

Companies to be ordered to proceed at once to Washington.

GOOD POSITIONS GIVEN TO SOLDIERS WHO HAVE SEEN SERVICE.

JAS. B. GRANT,
Recruiting Officer.

GEORGE F. NESBITT & CO., Printers and Stationers

Opposite: On the 2nd of January, 1862, the 1st Connecticut Heavy Artillery was organized from elements of the state's infantry. One of the major concerns of the Lincoln administration was the protection of Washington, sitting squarely in a region rampant with Confederate sympathies. Of the many forts built around Washington, pictured here is Fort Richardson. The guns belong to the 1st Connecticut Heavy Artillery. The unit remained here until April 1862, when it accompanied General McClellan's army on a seaborne expedition to attack the Confederate capital at Richmond, in what was called the Peninsula Campaign.

Below: The Harpers Ferry raid cost John Brown two sons, both dead, and now he too would face his Maker. On December 2, 1859, in Charles Town, the unlucky abolitionist bravely faced a noose. He predicted with deadly accuracy that only blood would purge the nation's evils. Among the crowd that witnessed the execution of John Brown were Thomas J. Jackson, an eccentric professor at Virginia Military Institute at Lexington, who was destined to earn the nickname "Stonewall," and a young actor named John Wilkes Booth, who this day wore a borrowed uniform of the Virginia militia just to be able to attend the momentous event. Booth, though philosophically opposed to Brown's cause, nevertheless admired him for his strength of conviction.

Opposite top: After their victory at Manassas (Bull Run to the Yankees), the Confederates moved to Centreville along one of the main routes to Washington. They did not possess the great quantity of heavy ordnance that the Union boasted, so the Confederates placed painted logs along their Centreville fortifications to give the impression of heavy armament. They were called "Quaker guns."

Opposite bottom: In early 1862 the Confederates under Joe Johnston evacuated their Centreville fortifications and fell back to a line along the Rappahannock River. After reconnoitering the Centreville position and finding it empty, the Federals occupied the abandoned fortifications and inspected the work of the Confederates. This picture shows an inspection tour by Union soldiers and engineers. They found much of the defensive works to be of the make-do variety, and the Quaker guns invited a hearty laugh. What the Confederates lacked in materiel they made up for in sheer determination, as their Centreville critics would soon discover.

Above: One of the earliest and most significant victories for the United States was in the West, where Brigadier General Ulysses S. Grant, depicted quite fancifully on horseback at far left, seized Forts Henry and Donelson on the Tennessee and Cumberland rivers, respectively, in February 1862, with considerable help from Flag Officer Andrew H. Foote and his gunboats. This illustration shows an attack in the vicinity of Fort Donelson on February 15, though the fort itself was never directly assaulted, except by the United States Navy operating in the Cumberland River. The fighting on the 15th was principally an attempt by the Confederates to break out of their lines protecting the fort and their base at nearby Dover, Tennessee, followed by a counter-attack by the Federals to regain lost ground. The Confederates surrendered next day. The fall of these two important forts broke Confederate Albert Sidney Johnston's principal defensive line in the West and led to the Union's bloodless occupation of Nashville on February 25. The victory also hurled the name Grant into prominence. He was promoted to major general, and earned the nickname "Unconditional Surrender" for his demands to the Southerners in this campaign.

Opposite: They served of all ages. This young fellow, probably an orphan or runaway, served aboard a naval vessel, and although his tasks were menial he faced manly hardships and dangers. The general rule was that one gun on shore was worth three, maybe four in the boat, during combat. Buckets of sand were ever-present on deck. A new recruit soon discovered why. During a spirited engagement the decks became slippery with blood, and the sand provided traction.

Above: This small steamboat, the *Eagle*, worked the Ohio River from the Marietta, Ohio area north to Wheeling, Virginia, in the region of that state that later pulled away from the Old Dominion to become West Virginia. A "packet boat" traveled a regular route carrying passengers, freight and mail. During the war, many steamers were converted to military use by adding some layers of armor and a few guns. They also served as troop carriers.

Above: One of the great turning points in naval warfare occurred with the advent of iron plating on ships. They could thus withstand a far greater pounding than traditional wooden vessels. On March 9, 1862, in what has been called the birth of modern naval warfare, the iron plated, raft-like USS *Monitor* with revolving iron turret battled the ironclad *CSS Virginia* to a tactical draw at Hampton Roads, Virginia. The Confederate vessel was formerly the USS *Merrimack*, a frigate that had burned to the waterline and was abandoned when the U.S. Navy was forced to evacuate Norfolk, Virginia. Using the *Merrimack's* hull and engines, the Confederates built the *Virginia*. And even though an entirely new type of vessel emerged, most people refer incorrectly to the battle of the 9th of March as the clash between the *Monitor* and the *Merrimack*.

Opposite: This view of the deck of the USS *Monitor* shows its revolving turret. Inside the turret are two 11-inch Dahlgren smoothbore guns. The warship was designed and built by John Ericsson, a Swede. Encouraged by the *Monitor's* performance in the Hampton Roads battle, Ericsson embarked on other naval projects. Later vessels included two revolving turrets, and improved designs permitted better handling.

Left: Despite naval advances, the steam-powered workhorse of the Civil War remained the locomotive. Trains carried troops and supplies in abundant quantities, with rapid efficiency, so that the nature of warfare changed. From the first major battle of the war at Manassas back in '61 to the last battle in '65, trains played a role. Strategic planning revolved around where railroads ran, and major campaigns resulted from the presence of tracks and locomotives. Great effort was spent during the war by both sides in destroying the enemy's railroads and repairing their own. Engineers became so adept at their work that they could build or rebuild a "toothpick" bridge, similar to this one, in a matter of days.

Above: The most famous locomotive of the Civil War was the Confederate engine #3 on the Western & Atlantic line, named the *General*. It traveled regularly between Chattanooga and Atlanta. On April 12, 1862, while at a breakfast stop at Big Shanty, Georgia, a band of 21 Yankees, dressed in civilian clothes and led by James J. Andrews, seized the locomotive and raced north, hoping to destroy tracks and bridges along the way. The raid, immortalized in several books and movies as "The Great Locomotive Chase," provided high drama on the rails as Southern trainmen gave chase on foot, horseback, pole car and commandeered locomotives, until the Andrews Raiders abandoned their mission 80 miles away, near Ringgold, Georgia. All of the raiders were captured, but some later escaped or were exchanged as prisoners. Some of them, including Andrews, were tried, convicted, and hanged as spies. Survivors of the aborted raid received the first Medals of Honor ever issued by the U.S. Congress, for heroism "above and beyond the call of duty."

Opposite: Train tracks not only carried boxcars full of troops and materiel, but they could also be used to transport new, mobile weapons, such as this huge mortar mounted on a flatcar. Pictured is a 13-inch seacoast mortar. It could toss a 220 pound exploding shell almost two-and-a-half miles. This was the largest of the mortars. Others came in bore sizes of 5.8, 8 and 10 inches.

Overleaf top left: One of the most dramatic naval battles of the war occurred in the Mississippi River at Memphis on June 6, 1862. As spectators along the waterfront watched in awe, five Union ironclads and four rams, under Commodore Charles Davis, gave battle to a force of eight makeshift Confederate vessels under Captain James E. Montgomery. It was a lop-sided affair, the Federals mounting 68 guns to the Southerners' 28. The guns roared and there was plenty of ramming by both sides during the two hour engagement, which the Federals won. Three of the Confederate boats were destroyed, four were captured, and only one, the gunboat *Van Dorn,* managed to slip away.

Overleaf bottom left: One of the Federal boats that participated in the Battle of Memphis was the USS *St. Louis,* pictured here, which was later renamed the *Baron de Kalb*. The *St. Louis* was one of seven armored gunboats designed by Samuel Pook and built by James B. Eads. Designed for river operations, all seven of "Pook's Turtles," as they were called, were named after Mississippi and Ohio river ports: *Cairo, Carondelet, Cincinnati, Mound City, Pittsburg,* and of course *St. Louis*. For this reason they were also called "city class" vessels. Four were built in the St. Louis area and three at Mound City, Illinois.

Overleaf right: Admiral David Glasgow Farragut (1801-1870) contributed to the success of Union efforts in early 1862. Assigned to command the West Gulf Blockading Squadron by Navy Secretary Gideon Welles, Farragut was charged with capturing the significant port city of New Orleans, Louisiana. His force of 24 wooden vessels and 19 mortar boats gave battle to Forts Jackson and St. Philip, blocking the passage to New Orleans, on April 18, and after successfully passing them on the 24th, accepted the surrender of the city next day. In addition to the important city of Nashville, taken by the Federals in February, the Confederacy's largest city was now occupied by bluecoats.

Above: General McClellan's first major campaign with his 105,000-man Army of the Potomac, initiated after prodding by the Lincoln administration, was a seaborne invasion of the peninsula between the York and James rivers in Virginia. At the tip of this peninsula was Union-held Fortress Monroe; inland some 75 miles to the northwest lay Richmond – the object of the campaign. Everything the army needed was brought by water. During the course of the campaign (March to August) the Federals had several different bases. This is the one at White House Landing on the Pamunkey River, a tributary of the York.

Opposite: Confederate General Joseph E. Johnston (1807-1891) faced McClellan during the Peninsula Campaign. A Virginian by birth and classmate of Robert E. Lee at West Point, both Class of 1829, Johnston fought with conspicuous gallantry in the Seminole and Mexican wars. By the time of the Civil War, he was Quartermaster-General of the U.S. Army with a brigadier's star. He resigned his commission to join the Confederacy on April 22, 1861, only two days after Lee resigned. Even though Lee was a colonel at the time of his resignation, and thus outranked by Johnston in the U.S. Army, Lee was commissioned a general in the Confederacy to rank ahead of Johnston. Harboring no ill will toward Lee, it nevertheless set "Old Joe" at odds instantly with President Davis – though some claimed the animosity extended back to Mexican War days – and the bitterness between the two would rear its ugly head on numerous occasions during the war, mostly to the detriment of their common cause.

Above: After an incredibly slow start, a characteristic that would doom McClellan, his army finally reached the proverbial "gates of Richmond" by late May 1862. The Confederate commander, Johnston, came under pressure from President Davis to halt the Union advance on the capital city. A showdown was at hand. This photograph by George Barnard purportedly shows Union artillerymen at an unfinished redoubt, preparing for the big battle that might end the war.

Right: The big battle in McClellan's march on Richmond occurred May 31-June 1, 1862, at a place called Seven Pines (or Fair Oaks). With his army split by the rain-swollen Chickahominy River, McClellan was attacked by Johnston's army in what proved to be a small tactical victory for the Federals. Much of McClellan's force was not in the fight, because of the river, so the two sides were fairly evenly matched. The Federals had 5,000 casualties out of about 40,000 engaged, and the Confederates lost 6,100. Sketched here by Alfred R. Waud is a scene after the battle as the slain are being gathered for burial and the dead horses for burning. McClellan was horrified by the carnage, and became ever more restrained in his already cautious handling of the army.

Opposite: The most significant outcome of the battle, as time would tell, was the severe wounding of General Johnston that led to his replacement by Robert E. Lee, who at the time was serving as Jefferson Davis' military advisor. Lee's first order to the army he would soon lead to immortality in the annals of military history, was an order to withdraw. Some thought Lee was an unwise choice, due to his failure to establish a Confederate hold on mountainous western Virginia early in the war. He proved his critics wrong.

Right: Three weeks after assuming command, Lee's troops, which he styled the Army of Northern Virginia, still had their backs to Richmond, and Lee launched a campaign to sweep McClellan back from the gates of the capital. The terrain in this region of Virginia was very swampy and densely overgrown with trees and brush. Maneuvering troops was difficult, but McClellan also had a ponderous wagon train to contend with. Roads and bridges had to be repaired or rebuilt constantly. Evidence of this type of engineering work is offered in this photograph taken at the time of the campaign.

Above: Lee's Seven Days Campaign relieved pressure on the Confederate capital, instilled the Army of Northern Virginia with a winning spirit that would sustain it through grueling campaigns ahead, and marked Lee as a commander to be reckoned with in this war (though his emergence as a *great* leader would occur during the ensuing months, especially·during the Second Manassas Campaign). The one battle Lee should not have fought during the Seven Days was the campaign's last one, Malvern Hill, on July 1, 1862. Lee's assault on the strong Union position cost him 5,000 men. Two of these three Confederate soldiers of the 3rd Georgia Infantry – the archive caption doesn't state which ones – were killed at Malvern Hill.

Opposite: Lee's campaign of June 25-July 1, called the Seven Days, was successful in putting McClellan's army to flight. Battles were fought at Mechanicsville, Gaines' Mill, Savage Station, Frayser's Farm, Malvern Hill. The campaign was a costly one, with Lee reporting over 20,000 casualties and McClellan about 16,000. This photograph by James Gibson of the Brady firm shows a field hospital at Savage Station.

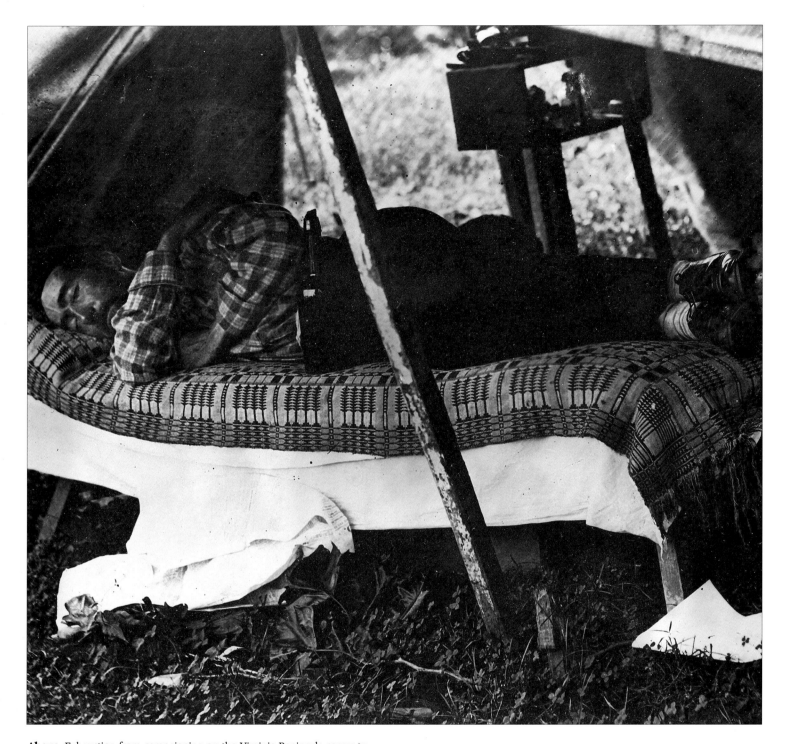

Above: Exhaustion from campaigning on the Virginia Peninsula seems to have affected many officers and men. Caught snoozing here is Lieutenant Colonel Samuel W. Owen of the 3rd Pennsylvania Cavalry. His unit was in the campaign from the beginning, participating in the siege of Yorktown in April, the Seven Pines battle of May 31-June 1, and back down the Peninsula in June and July. But there was little time for rest. New campaigns were beginning, and troops were marching out of Washington into northern Virginia to take advantage of the main Confederate army (Lee's) being posted over a hundred miles away in the Richmond area.

Opposite: Wherever the armies went in the South, there were sure to be Negroes who would attach themselves to Union columns or flee in the path of advancing Confederate legions. In Virginia this proved to be a near constant, back-and-forth business. This photo by Timothy O'Sullivan, who was employed by Mathew Brady, is described as fugitive Negroes fording the Rappahannock River in anticipation of the approach of Stonewall Jackson's men in August 1862. Jackson's participation in the Seven Days was a lackluster performance, generally attributed to exhaustion from his earlier campaign in the Shenandoah Valley.

Above: Hopes for success in the newest campaign of the Lincoln government rested on the shoulders of Major General John Pope, brought east after successes won in opening the Mississippi River. Pope's force consisted of the several independent commands that had operated unsuccessfully against Jackson in the Shenandoah, now consolidated as the Army of Virginia. Pope's performance against Lee's victory-flushed army brought up from the Peninsula was a disastrous affair, culminating in another embarrassing Union defeat along a familiar estuary. The Battle of Second Bull Run (or Second Manassas to the Confederates, who were inclined to name battles after towns rather than landmarks), like the first battle along this stream, ended with Union troops once again high-tailing down the same roads to the capital. It was another heart-breaking defeat for the boys in blue, and Lee's army continued to hold sway in the East.

Right: One of the personal embarrassments to Pope even before his campaign got underway was the capture of his baggage – personal papers and all. It occurred on a stormy Friday, August 22, when Jeb Stuart's Rebel horsemen struck Catlett's Station on the Orange & Alexandria Railroad. Among the trophies carried off by Stuart's men, in addition to hundreds of horses and mules and chests full of money, were Pope's hat and coat, one of his dress uniforms and his order book. This photograph shows Union troops repairing the track at Catlett's Station.

Above: After the successful reduction of Harpers Ferry, and a bloody delaying battle that had been fought in the passes of South Mountain on September 14, Lee was able to concentrate his army in and around Sharpsburg, Maryland for a showdown battle with McClellan, who by chance had obtained a copy of Lee's orders for the invasion. With his back to the Potomac River, Lee prepared to give battle along the banks of Antietam Creek, pictured here.

Opposite top: Their spirits buoyed by yet another success against Yankee arms, the Army of Northern Virginia launched an invasion of the North. The Maryland (or Antietam) Campaign began on September 4, 1862 when the Southern army crossed the Potomac River into Maryland. Lee hoped to take the war away from Virginia during harvest time, as well as to increase his ranks with Marylanders. And there was always the hope that a great victory on Northern soil would gain European recognition and aid for the Confederacy. Depicted in this sketch is Stonewall Jackson's command wading the Potomac at White's Ford. Lee was again pitted against McClellan, who had absorbed Pope's command into his own. Pope was sent to Minnesota to fight Indians.

Opposite bottom: Situated at the confluence of the Potomac and Shenandoah rivers was Harpers Ferry, a key objective in Lee's northward invasion. At the time, Harpers Ferry was garrisoned by over 10,000 Federals. Charged with capturing the place was Stonewall Jackson. Harpers Ferry had already changed hands a number of times in the war, and in 1859 it had been the scene of John Brown's raid, so violence seemed to haunt the town. By late summer of 1862, hardly anyone lived there anymore. Evidence of the destruction wrought upon the Ferry is the burned railroad bridge over the Potomac, viewed here from the Maryland side looking toward Harpers Ferry. After a two-day siege, the Union garrison at Harpers Ferry surrendered to Stonewall Jackson on September 15.

Above: The battle opened at dawn on September 17, with Federal troops under Major General Joseph Hooker, the First Corps of the Army of the Potomac, emerging from the North Woods into the 40-acre cornfield of the Miller farm. Depicted here is General Hooker, mounted on a white horse, directing the attack. Miller's cornfield would go down in history as a slaughter pen as Hooker's men struck Stonewall Jackson's line.

Opposite: As Hooker's troops battled across Miller's cornfield, leaving nearly every stalk of ripened corn cut down by gunfire, the Federals pushed on toward tiny Dunker Church at the edge of the West Woods along Hagerstown Pike. More bloodshed occurred around the church when Hooker's men were assailed by troops under Brigadier General John Bell Hood, who in turn were struck by the arriving Union Twelfth Corps under Major General Joseph K.F. Mansfield. Casualties mounted at an alarming rate, and included Mansfield, mortally wounded trying to rally his troops.

Above: These dead Confederates are very likely Louisiana troops of Stonewall Jackson's command. The view is looking north, toward the direction of Hooker's attack. The roadway at left is a farm lane, and the main pike connecting Hagerstown and Sharpsburg is on the other side of the high rail fence, which many of the unfortunate Rebels had tried to use for cover. The photo was taken by Alexander Gardner of the Brady company two days after the battle. It and others he took this day were the first ones to capture photographically the true carnage of a Civil War battle. Although the buying public was aghast at such scenes, Brady nevertheless sold hundreds.

Opposite top: The closing drama in the battle was the belated attack by Major General Ambrose E. Burnside's men at the Lower Bridge across the Antietam, on the southern portion of the battlefield. If all of McClellan's corps had attacked in concert, Lee might easily have been crushed. But that was not the case, allowing Lee to shift troops to meet each new threat. As luck would have it this day, no sooner did Burnside force the creek than Confederate reinforcements, arriving in the nick of time and literally prodded at the point of Major General A.P. Hill's sword, struck Burnside and saved the day for Lee. The bridge here was later named for General Burnside.

Opposite bottom: The Battle of Antietam (or Sharpsburg, as the Confederates called it) proved to be the war's bloodiest single day of combat. Some 25,000 Americans in blue and gray were casualties of the fighting on September 17, 1862. Though outnumbered two to one, Lee managed to stave off disaster and was able to get his mangled army back across the Potomac into Virginia. Pictured here is a hospital on the outskirts of the battlefield where the surgeon of a Union regiment, Dr. Anson Hurd, is tending to enemy wounded left on the field when the Confederates departed on the night of September 18-19.

Overleaf: Left in possession of the field, McClellan's army went into camp to rest and refit. The successful repulse of Lee's invasion gave President Lincoln his long awaited moment of victory to issue the Emancipation Proclamation. He also hoped that McClellan would give chase to the Confederates to deliver a finishing blow, but such was not to happen. Lincoln paid the general a visit in October, on the Antietam field where McClellan was still camped, and it was during this time that the photo here and the one following were taken by Gardner. Lincoln at six feet four inches towers over "Little Mac," sixth from the left. The fellow at far right is Captain George Armstrong Custer.

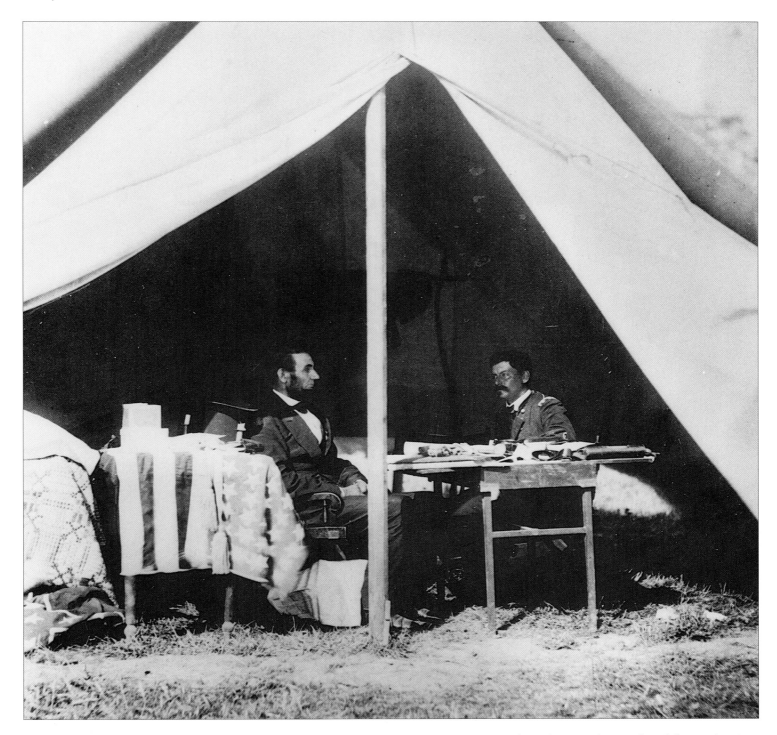

Above: On October 4 Lincoln met with General McClellan one last time before departing for Washington. The president was very concerned that the general had missed an opportunity to end the war by not pursuing Lee's crippled army. Alexander Gardner managed to capture the quiet drama of the moment. On the ground at left is a captured Rebel flag. After Lincoln left he continued to fret over McClellan's lack of aggressiveness, until November 7, when he relieved him. And so ended the military career of George B. McClellan, the "boy wonder" who was also styled "Young Napoleon." He was not yet 36 years old.

Opposite: Replacing McClellan in command of the Army of the Potomac was Ambrose E. Burnside (1824-1881). A West Point graduate (1847), Burnside left the army in 1853 to go into business for himself, manufacturing a breech-loading rifle of his own design, which turned out to be an unsuccessful enterprise. Oddly enough, not long before the war broke out he was working for his friend McClellan at the Illinois Central Railroad. Burnside's greatest qualities were his likable personality and perseverance, and he is perhaps best known for the bushy side-whiskers that still today are called "sideburns."

Opposite top: For over two weeks the armies stared at each other across the Rappahannock at Fredericksburg-Falmouth. Finally, on the foggy morning of December 11, Burnside sent his engineers down to the river with the pontoons, and in the face of Confederate sharpshooters on the Oppositebank the Federals began laying the bridges. It was dangerous work, but the bridges were soon in place and on the 12th the Army of the Potomac crossed over into Fredericksburg and prepared to give battle. This sketch shows Rebel pickets who gave their lives contesting the crossing.

Opposite bottom: Within days of assuming command of the Army of the Potomac, Burnside had it moving at a vigorous pace in pursuit of the Confederates. The advance was so swift and well executed that Lee was placed at a disadvantage when, on November 19, Burnside's entire army was massed at Falmouth, Virginia, on the Rappahannock River, overlooking the lightly defended town of Fredericksburg (pictured here, viewed from the Falmouth side of the river). Burnside's advantage was frittered away, however, when he insisted on waiting for pontoon bridging to arrive instead of forcing a crossing of the river. By the time the bridges arrived on November 25 the Confederates were dug in on the high ground at Fredericksburg.

Above: General Burnside's early Civil War career was marked with considerable success. His well-handled expedition to North Carolina in the spring of 1862 gave the Federals a coastal base from which to operate, and resulted in the capture of several important towns and one major installation, Fort Macon. This sketch, entitled "Traveling in State," depicts Burnside in his North Carolina victory days, traveling by hand car between New Bern and Beaufort, the latter place being the locale of Fort Macon. Postwar, Burnside was three-time governor of Rhode Island and was serving as U.S. Senator from that state when he died in 1881.

from Battle field

Above: Burnside's main assault occurred on December 13. Shown here are troops of Brigadier General Orlando B. Willcox's corps waiting amid the debris and looted trophies of Fredericksburg for the order to advance. In one of the most brutal assaults of the war, Burnside's men dashed in wave after wave against well-protected Confederates on high ground behind the city. Seeing his men slaughtering Yankees in wholesale fashion, the mild-tempered Lee pondered the awful grandeur of war. Another Confederate thought that not even a chicken could live long on the frozen plain stretching out from the Confederate position.

Opposite top: When all was said and done, Lee had racked up another stunning victory. The Battle of Fredericksburg was extremely costly to the Yankees. Of Burnside's estimated 130,000 men, nearly 13,000 were casualties. Most of them fell before the Confederates' position behind a stone wall along the rim of Marye's Heights on the northern end of the battlefield. Many wounded soldiers froze to death during the night as they lay exposed on the battlefield where they fell. Next morning, white bodies dotted the plain, the ill-clad Rebels having taken the uniforms of the dead during the night. Burnside pulled his men back to the Falmouth side of the river on December 15. Lee's losses in the battle numbered about 5,000 of his force of 75,000. Pictured here is the destroyed railroad bridge over the Rappahannock, with men of the two opposing armies staring across at one another.

Opposite bottom: This sketch, from a painting, shows Union troops arriving in Fredericksburg. In order to get the last pontoons laid, a small force had made an amphibious assault to clear the Oppositebank. Meanwhile, Federal artillery opened up on the town and shattered many historic buildings to rubble. As skirmishers inch their way forward, rooting out Confederate resistance, some of the town's finest old structures are engulfed in flames. Providing much of the resistance to the Union advance were sharpshooters from William Barksdale's Mississippi brigade.

137

Above: General Burnside was extremely distraught over the loss at Fredericksburg. The men were demoralized and no longer had any faith in their commander. When the Army of the Potomac was offered to him, Burnside had in fact expressed doubts over his ability to handle such a huge command. His shortcomings were all too plain now, and in an attempt to redeem himself Burnside planned a winter offensive. He hoped to march his army several miles upriver from Fredericksburg, cross the Rappahannock undetected, and strike Lee's rear. The march got underway on January 19. The weather took a wicked turn and the resulting trek back to camp after the offensive was called off was a horrible experience for all involved. The affair became known as "Burnside's Mud March," depicted here in a drawing by Alfred R. Waud.

Opposite: In the Western Theater of the war, Confederate General Braxton Bragg (1817-1876) was the principal character for the first half of the war. A West Point graduate and veteran of the Seminole and Mexican wars, he was irascible, uncompromising and possessed of eccentricities that made him utterly unapproachable except by long-time intimates. His friendship with President Davis assured Bragg's continued participation in military affairs, despite a lackluster performance. After a well-executed thrust into Kentucky during the late summer and fall of 1862, that took Rebel soldiers almost to the Ohio River at Cincinnati, Bragg then began bickering with fellow officer General Edmund Kirby Smith, and the two became preoccupied with Kentucky politics. Thus, the campaign stalled. The invasion was turned back at the Battle of Perryville on October 8, 1862.

Opposite top: Rosecrans' first battle with his new command was at Murfreesboro, Tennessee, along the banks of Stones River, where his army was assailed by Braxton Bragg's Confederates on December 31, 1862. The hard-fought contest lasted into the new year and resulted in a Union victory. Some of the bitter fighting is depicted in this drawing. The superiority of Union artillery carried the day. Bragg withdrew from the field on January 3.

Opposite bottom: Rosecrans' victory in the Battle of Stones River (or Murfreesboro) was a great boost to Union morale as the first full year of the war drew to a close. Pictured here is a Brady photograph of railroad repair in progress in the Murfreesboro area. Rosecrans' army wintered at Murfreesboro and turned the place into a fortified depot. Rosecrans became so comfortable here that come spring the Federal high command almost had to pry him out of the place to go after Bragg.

Above: Despite the Union victory at Perryville, the army commander, Major General Don Carlos Buell, was relieved for being too cautious and not providing adequate leadership during the battle. His replacement was William Starke Rosecrans (1819-1898), an Ohio native, graduate of West Point, and a very capable engineer officer. He is pictured here as a brigadier, though at the time he assumed command of Buell's army Rosecrans was a major general. His three corps were designated the Army of the Cumberland. Well liked by his men, he was nicknamed "Old Rosy."

Above: Shown here is the USS *Cairo,* one of the "Pook turtles" built by James B. Eads and a sister ship to the previously pictured *St. Louis.* On December 12, 1862, in one of the last naval expeditions of the year, the *Cairo* and four other gunboats involved in operations against Vicksburg, Mississippi, started up the Yazoo River. The Confederates had mined the river with their so-called "torpedoes" (mines). The *Cairo* struck two of them and sank in less than 15 minutes. (The gunboat has since been salvaged and is on display at Vicksburg.) Of related interest, the famed USS *Monitor,* while being towed along the North Carolina coast on December 30, 1862, sank in heavy seas off Cape Hatteras.

Opposite: He was seemingly invincible. His army was ill-clad and underfed but seemed to achieve the impossible. Richmond was not the conquest needed to end the Confederacy, for the lifeblood of the fledgling nation was not its capital city, but rather its armies. And the Army of Northern Virginia carried on its bayonets the hope of a people who cared less for preserving human bondage than for the concept of their own freedom and independence. Robert E. Lee (1807-1870) embodied that spirit.

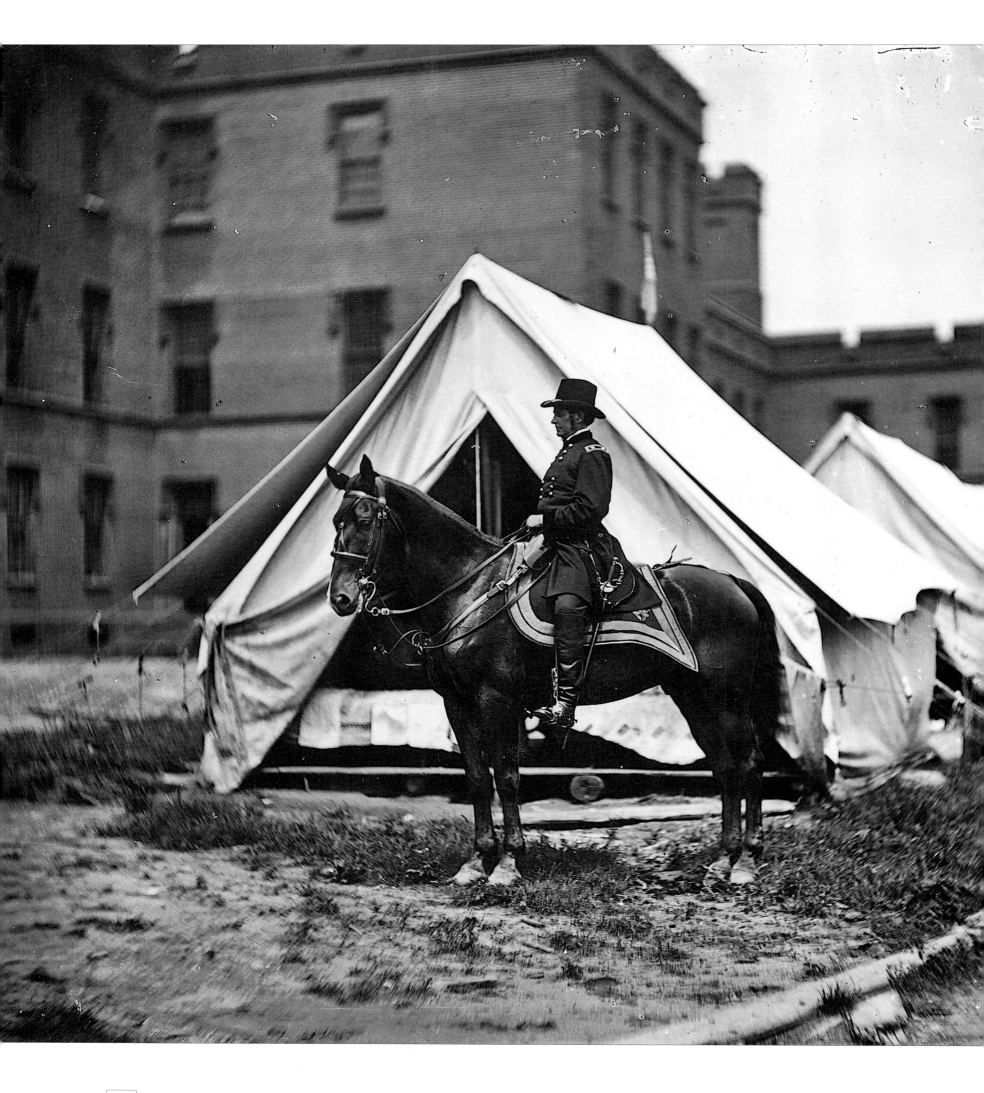

Opposite: One of Ambrose Burnside's most ardent critics was this man, Major General Joseph Hooker (1814-1879). When Lincoln cast about for a replacement commander for the Army of the Potomac, he settled on "Fighting Joe," who once said the country needed a dictator. Lincoln warned Hooker that he hoped the same back-stabbing that hampered Burnside's tenure in command would not affect Hooker – who had been one of the back-stabbers. Time would tell. Hooker was a native of Massachusetts, attended West Point, and served with distinction in the Mexican War. He was a hard fighter, headstrong and quite competent, but gained his nickname when a dash (or comma) was omitted between the word "Fighting" and his name in a telegraph message. Nevertheless, the name stuck and was rather appropriate based on past performance.

Below: The Army of the Potomac was in a critical state of demoralization when Hooker assumed command in January 1863. Not only was there the problem of the Fredericksburg debacle and subsequent Mud March, but many of the rank and file resented the war being turned into a moral crusade with the Emancipation Proclamation that took effect on January 1. But with the new year, a new commander, and soon the springtime, there was a rejuvenation. Hooker broke up Burnside's "Grand Divisions" into individual corps, reorganized the cavalry, instituted unit badges to promote *esprit de corps*, and his habitual drinking and swearing and aggressive nature made him popular with the men. The smiling faces of these men of the 61st New York Infantry, taken at Falmouth in March 1863, reflect renewed hope.

Opposite: Hooker's plan to defeat Lee involved dividing his army into thirds. While one third, under Major General John Sedgwick, held Lee's attention on the old Fredericksburg front, another third marched upriver, crossed the Rappahannock and got in Lee's rear, while the remaining third acted as a reserve. It was a brilliant move, executed without a hitch, and Hooker had placed Lee in a perilous situation. All "Fighting Joe" had to do was maintain the initiative and press his advantage. Meanwhile, Lee too split his army, leaving 10,000 men under Major General Jubal Early at Fredericksburg, and with the rest went to confront Hooker at Chancellorsville. Pictured here is Early's position – the same stone wall defended the previous December – after Sedgwick's attack forced the Confederates' withdrawal.

Below: This photograph has been mislabeled countless times in books and magazines. Generally captioned as an 1864 view of men under fire in the trenches about Petersburg, it is actually a portion of Hooker's army (Brooks' division of Sedgwick's Sixth Corps) entrenched along the banks of the Rappahannock River in May 1863, during the Chancellorsville Campaign.

Opposite: This damaged caisson is a relic of the Chancellorsville Campaign and fairly represents the shattered hopes of the Army of the Potomac. After stealing a march on Lee, Hooker lost control of himself and the campaign. This was variously attributed to the "shakes," Hooker having recently sworn off alcohol, or a severe concussion caused by a shell striking a column of the Chancellor house against which the general was leaning, or extreme command anxiety – or a combination of these factors.

Right: Another reason for Hooker's defeat at Chancellorsville was the audacious handling of the Army of Northern Virginia by General Lee, who boldly split his army several times in the face of a superior foe. The *coup de main* of the battle was a flank attack by Stonewall Jackson's men that crumbled the Federal line. This famous lithograph depicts Lee (left) and Lieutenant General Jackson conferring just before the flank march. It was their last meeting.

Below: The Battle of Chancellorsville, depicted in this Currier and Ives lithograph, was considered Lee's greatest victory. Indeed, the fluid movements of the army in the capable hands of Lee and Jackson, while facing superior numbers at every turn, demonstrated a supreme confidence in the army itself, from general down to private, and especially in the commanding generals, whom the men would follow anywhere through any hell of battle. The result was that Chancellorsville was a near-perfect offensive after the Confederates were initially placed at a distinct and potentially disastrous disadvantage. The Confederates lost some 13,000 men, but inflicted 17,000 casualties on the Federals. The only development that cast a shadow upon Lee's success was the wounding of the mighty Stonewall at the peak of the flank attack. He was accidentally shot by his own men, had his arm amputated, and died a short time later from complications. On the Federal side, Hooker was soon relieved and replaced by Major General George G. Meade.

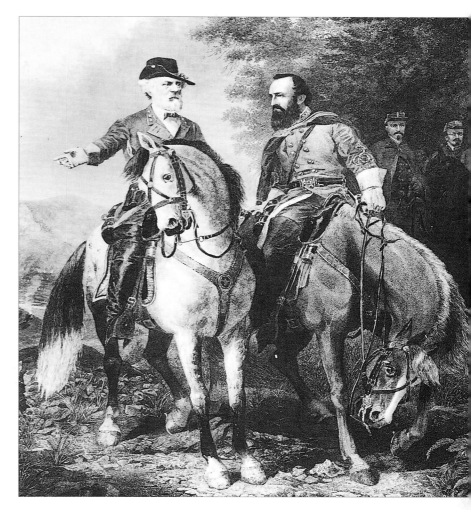

Above: By 1863 only Port Hudson, Louisiana, and Vicksburg, Mississippi, remained as Confederate strongholds on the Mississippi River. Both came under siege during the year. Beginning in March, Port Hudson came under fire in a siege that would last beyond the fall of Vicksburg. Depicted here is likely the June 14, 1863 attack on Port Hudson by Major General Nathaniel P. Banks' Army of the Gulf, supported by a naval flotilla. Banks failed to dislodge the stubborn garrison under Major General Franklin Gardner.

Left: This map shows the Vicksburg area and its defenses. Major General Ulysses S. Grant's first campaign against the fortified town on the Mississippi lasted from mid-October to mid-December of 1862. It failed for numerous reasons, not the least of which was a tenuous supply line, vulnerable to Confederate cavalry raids. Grant's second campaign against Vicksburg, after failures at the Battle of Chickasaw Bluffs (December 27-29, 1862) and on the Yazoo Pass and Steele's Bayou expeditions (February-March 1863), began in April. Grant had to contend with two Confederate forces in Mississippi, one under Lieutenant General John C. Pemberton at Vicksburg, and another under General Joe Johnston in the vicinity of the Mississippi state capital at Jackson.

Opposite: Confederate Major General James Ewell Brown "Jeb" Stuart (1833-1864), famed commander of Lee's cavalry, was a Virginian, West Point graduate, and veteran of Indian fighting on the Kansas frontier. Early in the war Stuart carved a niche for himself as a flamboyant and reckless cavalier by riding completely around McClellan's army on the Peninsula, launching sudden attacks on Union installations during rainstorms, and generally doing the unexpected. Continued success encouraged similar or more daring exploits. Despite his flair for the reckless and unpredictable, Stuart was a master at reconnaissance and in screening the army's movements. During the Battle of Chancellorsville, after both Jackson and A.P. Hill were wounded, it was Stuart, the horseman, who took temporary command of Jackson's infantry corps. At the beginning of the Gettysburg Campaign, Stuart was embarrassed by a surprise attack on his position at Brandy Station on June 9, 1863. Only after hard fighting and luck did Stuart salvage a tactical victory over the Potomac army's horsemen.

Above: This depiction of the Siege of Vicksburg is perhaps a bit too tidy, but nevertheless shows the town in the distance and the typical fortifications and siege lines surrounding it. Federal artillery drove residents from their homes to the shelter of caves. Hunger and disease took a dreadful toll on civilians and the 20,000-man Confederate garrison.

Right: With the death of Stonewall Jackson in May, his Second Corps was divided and given to Lieutenant Generals Richard S. Ewell (Second Corps) and A.P. Hill (Third). James Longstreet (1821-1904), pictured here, commanded Lee's First Corps and had earned the reputation as Lee's "War Horse," as well as the more endearing sobriquet "Old Pete." Born in South Carolina, Longstreet was the only non-Virginian in the corps command slots of Lee's army. It was Longstreet's belief that the Confederacy's best odds for success were to remain on the defensive and let the Yankees attack them. Lee and Longstreet would butt heads over strategy in the upcoming Gettysburg Campaign.

Opposite: Typical of the frustration and desperation along the Vicksburg siege lines was the exchange of "hand grenades" where the lines were close. This sketch by F.B. Schell, according to the archival caption, shows action during June 1863 between Confederate defenders and troops of Major General William T. Sherman. General Pemberton surrendered to Grant on July 4, 1863, and the Confederates were instantly paroled.

Previous pages : The opening clash in the Battle of Gettysburg was between Confederate infantry and dismounted Union cavalry. Pictured here is Captain John C. Tidball and men of Battery A, 2nd U.S. Artillery, taken in 1862. At the time of the Gettysburg Campaign, Tidball was commanding an artillery brigade in the cavalry corps of the Army of the Potomac, and it was one of his guns that fired the first artillery round of the battle.

Opposite: Cemetery Hill, just south of Gettysburg on Baltimore Pike, derived its name from Evergreen Cemetery. Pictured is the cemetery gatehouse. This high ground was the rallying point for Union troops driven through town by Lee's men on the first day of the battle. Elements of the First Corps, which fought on the ridges west of town, assembled here after being forced to retreat. They carried the bulk of the fighting on July 1, and lost their commander, Major General John F. Reynolds, killed. Drawn to the hill from fighting north of Gettysburg was the Eleventh Corps under Major General Oliver O. Howard, who established his headquarters on Cemetery Hill.

Below: Lee's next, and what would be his last invasion of the North, brought his army to this Pennsylvania town. The view is looking east toward Gettysburg, along the pike leading from Chambersburg – the road of the initial Confederate advance on July 1, 1863. The wooded hill in the background is Culp's Hill, and the tall tree on the horizon at right marks Cemetery Hill. The battle opened along the ridges west of Gettysburg, where the photographer is standing.

Above: General George G. Meade's victorious Army of the Potomac lost over 3,000 men killed and some 14,500 wounded in the three-day Battle of Gettysburg. Pictured here are Union dead at the Rose farm, casualties of the fighting on July 2. This photo is generally mislabeled as casualties of the first day's fighting, but recent studies pinpoint the Rose farm, where Georgians and South Carolinians struck Joseph Brooke's brigade of the Union Third Corps.

Opposite top: The dramatic charge for which Gettysburg is best known occurred on July 3, when, in a last-ditch effort to break the Federal position along Cemetery Ridge, Lee sent 11 brigades in an attack spearheaded by Major General George E. Pickett's division, just arrived on the battlefield. Though called "Pickett's Charge," his all-Virginia unit was but one of three divisions heavily involved, plus a fourth only partially engaged. The charge proved a lost gamble for Lee and his gallant Army of Northern Virginia.

Opposite bottom: On July 2, 1863, the second day of fighting at Gettysburg, the Confederates attempted to wrest Cemetery Hill from its Union defenders. The day had seen some of the bloodiest fighting of the war, most of it along the southern end of the field, in the vicinity of the Peach Orchard, Wheatfield, and Little Round Top. But on the evening of the 2nd, two Rebel brigades lurched forward into the twilight and charged Cemetery Hill, temporarily seizing a part of the lines until Union reinforcements pushed them back down the slopes.

Above: On July 2, Confederate troops from Alabama swept into the valley cut by Plum Run, between Devil's Den – a nest of huge boulders – and the base of the highest hill in the vicinity, Round Top, only to find themselves in a hot contest that earned the place the name "Slaughter Pen." This fellow, very likely a member of the 44th Alabama Infantry, did not survive.

Opposite: This sniper's nest amid the boulders of Devil's Den was used by the Confederates to pick off Union officers on Little Round Top, 600 yards away. The photographer and his helpers dragged the corpse of this Texas or Georgia infantryman into the nest so the image could be entitled "A Sharpshooter's Last Sleep." He was actually killed 40 yards away. An exhaustive study of the photographs of Gettysburg by an expert in the field of Civil War photography revealed the secrets in this view, and evidences the intense and enduring interest in the battle by historians.

Opposite: Gettysburg statistics showed that each side lost over 5,000 men listed as missing, presumed captured. This photo of three Confederate prisoners is one of the most famous of the war, and captures the essence of the typical Confederate soldier in Lee's army. There is hardly any trace of a uniform and the fellows have a rugged look of no-nonsense about them. The picture was taken on Seminary Ridge.

Above: These Confederates were killed at the Rose farm on July 2, during the fight with the fellows three pictures back. The Southern boys were from Brigadier General Paul J. Semmes' brigade – he himself was mortally wounded here – and were members of either the 15th South Carolina or 53rd Georgia. A host of photos were taken at the Rose farm by cameramen Timothy O'Sullivan, James Gibson and Alexander Gardner.

Left: In November 1863 President Lincoln came to Gettysburg to participate in a ceremony to dedicate the soldiers' cemetery established adjacent to Evergreen Cemetery. Thousands of people poured into town to hear the foremost orator of the day, Edward Everett, and listen to a few remarks from the president. As it turned out, Everett spoke for two hours, Lincoln fewer than five minutes. But the president's "Gettysburg Address" has been memorized by school children for over a century. No one remembers anything of Everett's speech.

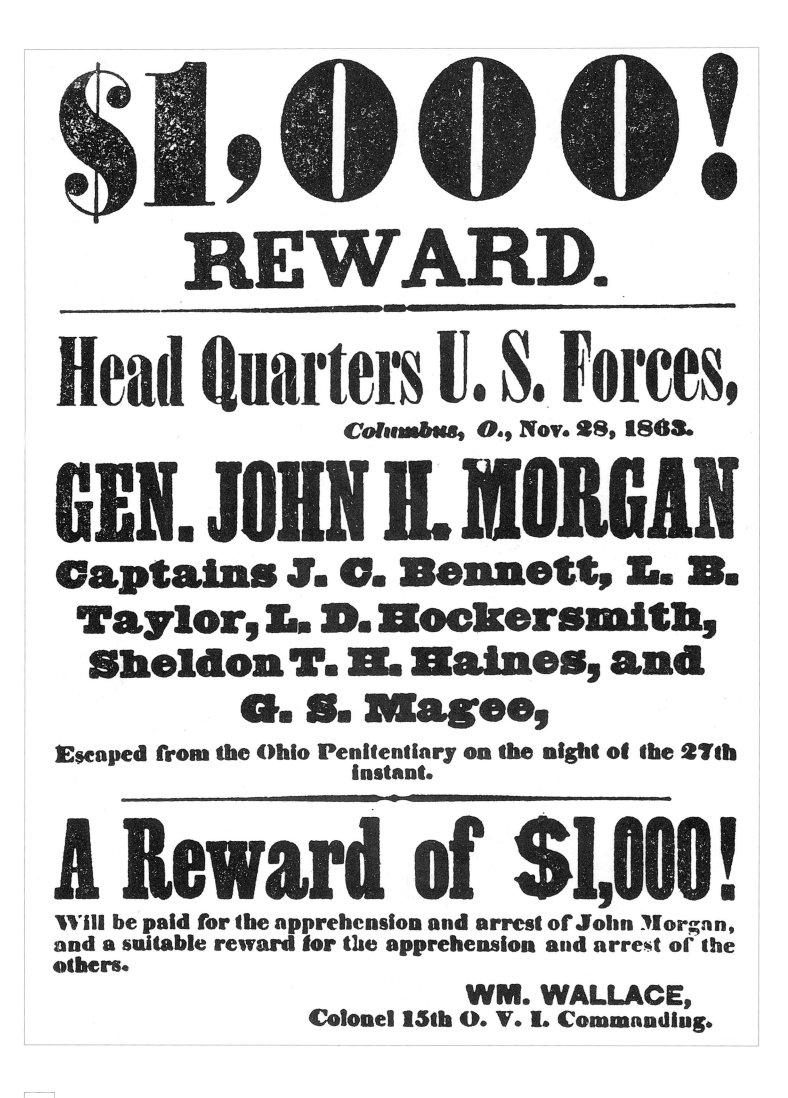

Opposite: July 1863 was an exciting month: Gettysburg, Vicksburg, Port Hudson, Battery Wagner, and the raid of Confederate Brigadier General John Hunt Morgan into Ohio. While Southerners were saddened by the news of Lee's defeat and the fall of Vicksburg, they rejoiced over headlines proclaiming that Morgan was taking the war to the North. His men burned and plundered, fought numerous skirmishes and one pitched battle, and captured or otherwise held the attention of countless thousands of Union and Northern militia troops. Morgan and the remnant of his command were captured July 26 in eastern Ohio, just a few miles shy of the Pennsylvania line. Because of the fear and consternation generated by the raid, Morgan and some of his principal officers were not sent to prisoner of war camps, but rather to the Ohio State Penitentiary in Columbus, where they were treated as criminals. As the reward poster states, Morgan escaped the following November. Making it safely back to Confederate territory, he raised a new force and raided some more, until his death in September 1864.

Left: Join the army, receive a bounty of $300, and above all – avoid the draft! The North's first conscription act was passed on March 3, 1863. All male citizens between the ages of 20 and 45 were liable for enrollment, except those who were mentally or physically unfit. A man called up in the draft could hurry off and enlist and gain a bounty, or hire a substitute, or buy his way out for $300. Rather than sign up, he might also take to the hills and hide for the rest of the war. Figures show that the draft encouraged volunteering.

Below: Even though the nation was at war with itself, immigrants nevertheless poured into the country, providing the North with a steady pool of manpower. Over 800,000 people came to America during the war, mostly from Germany (almost a quarter-million) and Ireland (a fraction below 200,000). In 1863, the year of conscription and draft riots, 176,000 foreigners arrived on the Northern shore. This sketch shows recruiters enlisting Germans and Irish on the Battery at New York City.

Above: With half of the Union army shattered and in flight, total disaster was avoided at Chickamauga only by a heroic stand on Snodgrass Hill by troops under this man, Major General George H. Thomas (1816-1870). Born in Virginia, he graduated from West Point in 1840, in a class that included William T. Sherman. Like most of his peers, Thomas fought in the Seminole and Mexican wars. At the outbreak of the Civil War, Thomas stayed with the Union, earning the disaffection of his sisters, who were staunchly aligned with the Southern cause of independence. For his stand on Snodgrass Hill, Thomas earned the nickname "Rock of Chickamauga."

Opposite top: With the passage of the conscription act in March, explosive demonstrations erupted across the land. The worst draft riots occurred in New York City in July. During three days of fighting between police and armed mobs, dozens were killed and hundreds more injured. Acts against the changing direction of the war, from one to save the Union to one to free the slaves, were notable. Blacks were lynched and Negro institutions burned. Troops fresh from the Gettysburg field were called in to restore order. Shown here is rioting on New York's 2nd Avenue.

Opposite bottom: In the West, the Confederacy won a stunning victory at the Battle of Chickamauga, September 19-20, 1863. Braxton Bragg's army, reinforced by part of James Longstreet's First Corps of Lee's army, delivered a drubbing to Rosecrans' Army of the Cumberland along Chickamauga Creek in northern Georgia. This sketch by J.F.E. Hillin shows some of the action.

Above: After the Battle of Chickamauga, Rosecrans' army fled to Chattanooga, where it soon became trapped by forbidding terrain, the twisting Tennessee River, and the presence of Braxton Bragg's Confederates. Lookout Mountain formed part of the trap, looming 1,100 feet over the town. A change in command was necessary, as Rosecrans seemed to have lost control of the situation. George Thomas was selected as the new commander of the Army of the Cumberland, and U.S. Grant, recently named chief of all armies in the West, arrived at Chattanooga to supervise matters. Within a short time supplies were flowing in at a rapid pace; Union troops battled up the slopes of Lookout Mountain (depicted here) and planted the Stars and Stripes at the crest; and Thomas' men swept Bragg's Rebels from Missionary Ridge. The siege was lifted, Bragg's army was put to flight, and Grant gained another feather in his cap.

Opposite: In the East, although the Army of the Potomac had followed Lee's beaten army into Virginia, things remained relatively quiet after Gettysburg. With 50,000 combined casualties in that battle, neither side was healthy enough to do more than rest and refit. Here, in August 1863, the drummers of the 93rd New York, veterans of Gettysburg, drill along the Rappahannock River in Virginia.

Above: By modern standards, the state of the medical art during the Civil War bordered on the primitive. This cozy scene belies the fact that most of these men are probably the lucky survivors of some battlefield hospital where an overworked surgeon wielded a knife and saw with dirty hands. Bloody bandages from a dead man might be torn away for reuse on a fresh victim. Little was known about the causes of infection.

Left: How long could the Confederacy last? Sure, its armies were still winning battles, but each battle, victory or no, cost the Southern nation men and materiel that were fast becoming irreplaceable. This cartoonist portrays a gaunt Jeff Davis, sickle in hand, reaping a harvest of death. Skulls, buzzards, a noose, and a threatening snake in the grass round out the symbolism. But the question remained: just how long could the Confederacy last?

Opposite: During 1863 a simmering feud within the photographic firm of Mathew Brady resulted in several skilled photographers severing their ties with the New York studio. Brady's eyesight was so bad that his employees had taken most, if not all of the battlefield photos, but every one carried Brady's name only – and the photographers resented it. Alexander Gardner left Brady and started his own firm, taking other professionals with him, like O'Sullivan and Gibson, on promise that their work would carry their own names. Indicated on the credit line of this photograph of a Union post office in the field, is the name T.H. O'Sullivan as the photographer who created the negative, and the name Gardner as the man who processed the positive.

50

Above: This Brady photograph captures the ambulance drill of the medical team attached to the 57th New York Infantry, called the "National Guard Rifles." With a record of participation in such battles as Antietam, Fredericksburg, Chancellorsville, and Gettysburg, the ambulance boys more than earned their pay. Generally, musicians doubled as hospital stewards and assisted with the ambulances. This regiment's loss during the war was 194 from all causes: killed, mortally wounded, or dead from disease.

Opposite: This fellow of the medical corps has a look in his eye like he can't wait to get his hands on a new patient. He's obviously concocting some mixture that may or may not be useful to the person he's attempting to make well again. All in all they did the best they could with the know-how and tools they possessed. But it was common knowledge that soldiers were nearly as frightened of surgeons as they were of the enemy. Especially in prisons, if you were admitted to the hospital you were all but conceding that your case was hopeless.

Above: One of the banner names of 1864 was that of William Tecumseh Sherman (1820-1891). Born in Ohio, young "Cump" Sherman went to live with the Thomas Ewing family, just up the street, when his father died and his mother was unable to support such a large household. Ewing was a U.S. Senator and Secretary of the Interior, and it was his daughter that Sherman later married; three of Ewing's sons became generals during the Civil War. Ewing got Sherman an appointment to West Point, from which he graduated sixth in his class in 1840. He missed the fighting in Mexico, being posted to California most of the time. After leaving the army in 1853, Sherman suffered through a dismal string of business failures, and was superintendent of a Louisiana military school when the Civil War started. After a shaky start in the war, during which he endured a period when many thought him insane, Sherman soon hit his stride and emerged as a brilliant commander with keen strategic insight.

Opposite: There were unsung heroes who kept the trains running, the paddle wheels churning and, of course, the ambulances in top shape. This shop, photographed by the Brady firm, was in Washington. Besides bullets, it was diarrhea, measles and smallpox, pneumonia, scurvy and a host of other diseases and afflictions that might land a fellow in the hospital. Indeed, more soldiers went under the sod from disease than from death or mortal wounding in battle. The Federal government imported most of its drugs during the war. The South too relied on imports, but the Union blockade of hostile ports kept the flow of needed medicines to a minimum.

Opposite: In the fall of 1864 a pontoon bridge was constructed on the Appomattox River at Broadway Landing to facilitate communication and supply between the City Point depot and Federal troops (the Army of the James) operating on the north side of the Appomattox, in an area known as Bermuda Hundred. Thus Broadway Landing, pictured here, became a satellite depot for the Federals, and this and other bridgeheads were extensively photographed in the fall and winter.

Above: With the coming of spring in 1864, Sherman moved into northern Georgia with three armies under him. Their target: Atlanta. Sherman's adversary was Joe Johnston, who had replaced Braxton Bragg after his resignation in the wake of the Chattanooga disaster of late '63. Skillful maneuvering through mountainous terrain caused Johnston to relinquish valuable territory, and to incur the wrath of President Davis. Late June found Johnston's Army of Tennessee posted along high ground known as the Kennesaw Line, named after the highest point, Kennesaw Mountain, which was actually comprised of Big and Little Kennesaw and a spur called Pigeon Hill. Sherman ceased maneuvering and ordered an all-out assault on the Confederate position on June 27. It was a costly, fruitless affair. This sketch shows artillery in action on the Kennesaw Line.

Above: After the Battle of Kennesaw Mountain, Sherman returned to his old game of flanking and maneuvered Johnston out of the Kennesaw position. Sherman was soon across the Chattahoochee River and well on his way to Atlanta. On July 17 Johnston was removed from command, for he failed to convince anyone in Richmond that he had a plan to deal with Sherman. The replacement was John Bell Hood (1831-1879), a Kentucky native, West Pointer, and best known in this war as a tough division leader under Robert E. Lee in the East, where Hood had made a name for himself early on, while in command of the famed Texas Brigade. His new home was with the Army of Tennessee, and now he commanded it.

Right: Hood was picked to command the Confederate army because he was known to be a fighter. Not overly smart, he knew the basics of his trade and had observed at first hand the battle-winning exploits of Stonewall Jackson and Robert E. Lee. Hood's first order was an attack, at Peachtree Creek, north of Atlanta, on July 20, 1864, where he failed to destroy a portion of Sherman's army. He attacked again two days later, east of Atlanta, but Sherman pressed onward, ever-tightening his grip on the city. Less than a week later, at the Battle of Ezra Church, Hood's best laid plans again went awry and he suffered severe losses. This George Barnard photo shows Sherman (leaning on the gun breech) and his staff on the outskirts of Atlanta.

Opposite: The key to Sherman's campaign for Atlanta was the rail network. Follow the railroads and you would inevitably find Sherman's men, either tearing up the tracks or trying to get to them for that purpose. His march into Georgia had been along the Western & Atlantic Railroad, which led from Chattanooga southward to Atlanta. Other railroads extended spider-like from Atlanta, making the city an important depot and transportation center for the Confederacy.

Below: There was a certain way Sherman wanted the rails destroyed. One simply did not pry them up and toss them away. The Rebels could fix them in no time at all. Sherman instructed his men to pile up railroad ties and set them on fire. Then, the rails were set across the burning ties so that the heat caused them to bend, rendering the rails useless. They were called "Yankee hairpins" or "Sherman's neckties."

Above: Despite Hood's best efforts, his army punched itself out in three sorties against Sherman's armies and lost much of its offensive ability. It was only a matter of time. A hard-fought battle at Jonesboro, south of Atlanta, on August 31-September 1, did Hood in. His army limped away to fight again, but on September 2, the mayor of Atlanta surrendered his city to Sherman's men. Before the Confederates left, they made sure that the Yankees would find little to use against them. Pictured here is what was left of the depot. Hood's entire ordnance train was blown up by retreating Rebels. (Movie buffs might take note that the well known scenes of a fiery Atlanta in the film version of Margaret Mitchell's best-selling novel of the Old South, *Gone With the Wind*, are often mistaken as Sherman's burning of Atlanta. But that event did not occur until November 1864. The conflagration in the movie, placed within a true historical setting and actual chronological sequence, is the blaze caused when Hood's ordnance train was set afire by the retreating Confederates.)

Opposite: Among the rubble of Atlanta's train station was the locomotive *General*, the one that Union raiders had attempted to steal back in '62. This famous locomotive was restored, and after the war made the rounds of fairs, expositions and veterans' reunions. Today the *General's* home is a museum at Big Shanty, Georgia, the old stop on the Western & Atlantic line where James Andrews and his raiders stole the locomotive.

Above: In November 1864 the final chapter of Atlanta's role in the war was written. Sherman put the torch to the city's war-making potential – a fire that spread from shops, factories and warehouses to private homes, churches and schools – and embarked on his March to the Sea. Essentially a change of base, it involved abandoning his tenuous supply line by rail up through northern Georgia, Tennessee and Kentucky. Sherman's men lived off the land and the civilian population until they reached the Atlantic coast, where the navy would become the new supply source. By Christmas, Sherman's men had taken Savannah. Pictured here are men of Sherman's Fifteenth Corps inspecting one of the big guns in Fort McAllister on the Ogeechee River, captured during operations against Savannah.

Opposite top: They thought he had been sent from Heaven. As Sherman's armies marched through Georgia, Negroes with all they owned, their families crammed into conveyances of every sort, or on foot, fell in behind the armies. Sometimes a burden, always a distraction, the caravan of Negro "contrabands" had to be dealt with if Sherman was to get on with the business of winning the war. During his advance on Savannah, Sherman burned a bridge behind him, stranding the pitiful refugees on the other side. It was Sherman who later delivered the famous "War is hell" speech, summing up all the grim necessities of conflict.

Opposite bottom: Back in Virginia a new day was dawning for the Union war effort. In March, Ulysses S. Grant was elevated to General-in-Chief of all Federal armies, with the revived rank of lieutenant general. Having left Sherman to command in the West – which he did admirably, successfully capturing Atlanta – Grant went east and made his headquarters with George Meade's Army of the Potomac. Grant prepared to match wits with the premier Confederate commander, Robert E. Lee. Their first engagement, in early May 1864, was a brutal affair in a tangle of brush and trees known as the Wilderness. In this sketch, Major General Gouverneur K. Warren, commanding the Union Fifth Corps, rallies his Marylanders during fighting in the Wilderness.

Contrabands escaping.

May 29th Hanover Town Va.

White House-
Ragged flag-

Genl Warren rallying the Marylanders

led. escaping from the burning woods of the Wilderness —

Above: One of the war's most horrible scenes, in a war full of awful spectacles, was the Wilderness catching fire during the battle. Wounded men watched in horror as flames licked closer and oppressive heat made breathing difficult. Informal truces were called so that men could be rescued from the inferno, regardless of the color of uniform.

Opposite: After the Battle of the Wilderness, May 5-7, 1864, and a series of bloody engagements around Spotsylvania Court House, May 8-19, the Confederates were convinced that this man Grant was different from any other commander they'd faced. Usually the Army of the Potomac retreated after a major battle to lick its wounds, refit and reorganize. That was no longer the case. Grant pounded away relentlessly, never letting Lee's army out of his grasp. This photograph is of a council of war at Massaponax Church on May 21. Pews have been hauled from the church into the yard to provide seating, and the photographer, Timothy O'Sullivan, has found a vantage point on the second story of the church. Grant can be seen at lower left, leaning over Meade's shoulder and pointing to a map in Meade's hands. They're discussing the pursuit of Lee's army southward.

Overleaf left: Bloodshed approached ghastly proportions during the fighting in the Wilderness and at Spotsylvania. Grant was criticized for his loss of men in what everyone viewed as a terrible war of attrition. Grant had a significant edge in manpower, so he could afford to play such a game. A victim of the fighting around Spotsylvania on May 19 was this Confederate soldier of Ewell's corps, photographed the day after his death by Timothy O'Sullivan. The soldier was killed on the Alsop farm, during a reconnaissance in force by two divisions of Ewell's corps that turned into a full-blown battle.

Overleaf right: Within a few yards of the dead soldier in the previous photo was this unfortunate fellow, that fact having been ascertained from another photograph taken a short distance away that shows both corpses. Scenes such as this must have captivated the buying public, or photographs of the dead would not have been as widely taken this late in the war. Where there was demand, men like Brady, O'Sullivan, Gardner and Gibson sought to create the necessary supply. Grant's campaign provided more than ample subjects, and this time the photos were taken in record time after death occurred.

Above: Pictured here is the wrecked bridge of the Richmond, Fredericksburg & Potomac Railroad over the North Anna River, about 25 miles north of Richmond. Fighting occurred in this area on May 23-26 as Grant's forces pursued Lee after breaking contact at Spotsylvania on the 19th. The railroad bridge was demolished in a joint effort, the Confederates having destroyed the southern end on May 23, and Federal troops finished the work on the 25th, along with tearing up track beyond the bridge. This photo, taken on the 25th, shows smoke still drifting up from the smoldering debris.

Opposite top: Despite the loss of several of his employees who had struck out on their own, Mathew Brady kept enough photographers in his stable to share in the lucrative picture-selling business. This photo of a burial scene at Fredericksburg in May 1864 was taken by a Brady man.

Opposite bottom: When Grant came east he brought Major General Philip H. Sheridan with him and placed Sheridan in command of the Army of the Potomac's cavalry corps. As Grant and Lee slugged it out at Spotsylvania, the cavalry of both sides ranged far and wide, and at Yellow Tavern on May 11, Sheridan's men mortally wounded Jeb Stuart. The glory days of the Virginia cavalry were over. A measure of revenge was achieved a month later when Sheridan's troopers were defeated in a battle at Trevilian Station, where the Confederate cavalry was commanded by Major General Wade Hampton, Stuart's successor.

Above: As the armies of Grant and Lee battled almost constantly, further to the west a Union command under Major General David Hunter was wreaking havoc in the Shenandoah Valley. To contend with this menace, some 14,000 Confederates under Lieutenant General Jubal A. Early (1816-1894) split from the main body of the Army of Northern Virginia and marched west to the Valley. A graduate of West Point in 1837, Early fought in the Seminole War and afterward resigned to study law, but reentered the service for the Mexican War. The word generally used in describing him is "crusty," and his grizzled appearance in this photograph seems to justify the adjective. Early was cool under fire and always a good fighter once in the fray.

Opposite: After the fighting along the North Anna River, and a slaughter of Grant's men in his ill-advised attack at Cold Harbor in the first days of June, the armies came to rest before Petersburg. This photograph, compliments of the Confederate Museum in Richmond, is of Private George W. Livesay, a member of a Petersburg artillery unit, who was killed August 18, 1864, probably during the fight along the Weldon Railroad south of Petersburg.

Left: With General Early in his expedition to the Shenandoah Valley was the 13th Virginia Infantry, whose flag is pictured. Early's operations against David Hunter's army in the Valley were so successful that Early decided to take his banner northward to threaten the lower Shenandoah Valley region and even the United States capital. On the way he won an important victory at the Battle of Monocacy, fought in Maryland on July 9, 1864. By the time Early reached the defenses of Washington on July 11 he found the fortifications manned by veterans sent north by Grant. President Lincoln was visiting the defenses at the time of Early's raid and briefly came under fire at Fort Stevens. On the 12th, Early withdrew from the Washington environs.

Below: The Army of the Potomac had sustained a staggering 50,000 casualties since the 1864 campaign began back in May at the Wilderness. Lee had never been pressed this hard before, and his losses were heavy as well. It was after the Battle of Cold Harbor, June 1-3, 1864, where Grant lost 7,000 men, that he realized his direct approach to Lee's army and the Confederate capital must be abandoned. Instead, the Federal commander consulted a map and traced his finger along the railroads feeding Richmond, and saw that four of the five lines ran through Petersburg. That's how this town 20 miles south of Richmond had become the newest target of operations. Earthworks, big guns, bombproofs. It could mean only one thing: siege, and it lasted almost ten months.

Opposite: The Federals brought this monster mortar to the Petersburg lines by flatcar. Nicknamed "Dictator," it was the largest weapon of its type used at Petersburg and arrived in position on July 9. According to contemporary accounts, the mortar itself recoiled only a couple of feet upon firing, while the flatcar would move three or four yards. After only five firings the platform broke. "Dictator" continued to serve along the Petersburg lines but never in a very decisive role and, as one photographic historian has noted, if the mortar had not been captured numerous times on photographers' plates for the oddity it was, the "Dictator's" role at Petersburg would probably have gone largely unnoticed.

Above: Life in the siege lines was incredibly boring, and extremely dangerous. This fanciful drawing, entitled "The Interrupted Game: Within the Intrenchments before Petersburg," appears to have been sketched by a fearless non-commissioned officer, for the sergeant resting on his musket is the only one not frightened by a huge, fizzing shell just landed – without indentation in the earth, by the way – in their trench, smack in the middle of their card game. In moments the thing could blow them all o kingdom come. A puff of smoke on the horizon indicates its origin. These "wicked" fellows might deserve everything that's coming to them. Card playing was considered evil by many, and soldiers were known to toss away their decks when going into battle. There are also obvious signs of drinking.

Opposite: City Point, Virginia, on the James River seven miles east of Petersburg, became Grant's headquarters and supply base. In a very short time, engineers built a sturdy new wharf, warehouses and a large hospital. Telegraph wire was run the length of the Peninsula to Fortress Monroe, providing Grant with a communication link to Washington and the rest of the war. Grant was, after all, in command of all of the armies of the United States, and he directed all the operations from here at City Point. Lincoln visited him here, and Sherman dropped in for a conference.

Above: On October 27, 1864 Grant extended his lines to the left (south and west) toward Hatcher's Run below Petersburg, inching ever closer to the South Side Railroad, the main supply artery for Lee's army. An estimated 43,000 Union soldiers were involved in the move. In what has been called the Battle of Burgess' Mill, or Boydton Plank Road, one of several engagements fought along Hatcher's Run, the Federals' advance was blunted by two divisions of Confederate infantry and Hampton's cavalry. The battle lasted until dark and Grant's lunge for the South Side was unsuccessful. This William Waud drawing shows the treatment of wounded in the woods after the battle.

Opposite: This Brady photograph shows but a fraction of the stockpile of materiel for Grant's army at City Point. For almost a year this obscure James River landing was one of the busiest places in the country, if not the world. Boats and barges came and went daily, bringing supplies and reinforcements for the front. One of the most dramatic moments at City Point occurred on August 9, 1864, when Confederate saboteurs exploded an ammunition barge, killing 43 and wounding 126. The commanding general himself narrowly escaped injury or death.

Overleaf top left: This 1864 photograph shows a Dahlgren gun crew on board the USS *Mendota*. The U.S. Navy employed nearly 70,000 men, and one in four worked in the shipyards. The Navy's strength in vessels grew from 90 at the beginning of the war to near 700 by war's end. The Federal government held a tremendous advantage over the Confederacy in naval resources. The Confederates had no ships at the outbreak of war, but managed by hook or crook to press all sorts of small steamers and sailing vessels into service as makeshift gunboats. A few significant purchases were made, such as the *Alabama* and *Shenandoah*.

Overleaf bottom left: In June 1864 the famous Confederate raider *Alabama,* under Raphael Semmes (a brother of General Paul J. Semmes, mortally wounded the previous year at the Rose farm outside Gettysburg), arrived at Cherbourg, France for resupply. Three days later the USS *Kearsarge* anchored outside the harbor to await the raider. The big sea battle took place on June 19 off Cherbourg, beyond the territorial limit. It lasted a little more than an hour, and when the smoke cleared the *Alabama* was going down. The *Kearsarge* took on 63 prisoners, while Semmes and many other officers and crewmen were rescued by a British yacht.

Overleaf right: Pictured here is John A. Winslow (third from left), captain of the victorious USS *Kearsarge*, with his officers after they sank the *Alabama*. Until its demise off the coast of France, the famed Confederate raider, built at Liverpool, England, had traveled nearly 75,000 miles and sunk, captured or burned over five dozen Federal ships. The *Kearsarge* mounted seven big guns, the *Alabama* eight, but the Confederate vessel was not in prime condition, having arrived at Cherbourg for an overhaul. Nevertheless, Winslow's victory was fairly won, and ended the *Alabama's* reign on the high seas.

Above: An important naval engagement in 1864 was the Battle of Mobile Bay, fought on August 5 along the Gulf coast in Alabama. The Union hero of the battle was Admiral David G. Farragut, pictured here (left) aboard his flagship, the *Hartford*, after the victory. Built at the Boston Navy Yard and launched in November 1858, the *Hartford* was 225 feet long and displaced 2,900 tons, drawing 17 feet. It mounted 20 9-inch Dahlgren guns, two 20-pounder Parrotts and two 12-pounders. In January 1862 the *Hartford* had become Farragut's flagship in his new job as commander of the West Gulf Blockading Squadron.

Opposite top: Here is another view of the crew of the *Mendota*. The U.S. Navy's biggest role in the Civil War was the blockade of Southern ports. It was estimated that at its peak, nearly 500 vessels and over 2,400 guns were involved in blockading activities along the 3,500 miles of Confederate coastline. The effectiveness of the blockade has long been a source of debate, but most agree it was worth the effort, if not decisive in the Union victory.

Opposite bottom: The entrance to Mobile Bay was protected by Forts Gaines, Morgan and Powell, along with numerous channel obstructions and torpedoes (mines), as well as Admiral Franklin Buchanan's Confederate flotilla of three gunboats and the ironclad *Tennessee*. Pictured here is Farragut's fleet of 14 wooden vessels and four monitors entering the bay.

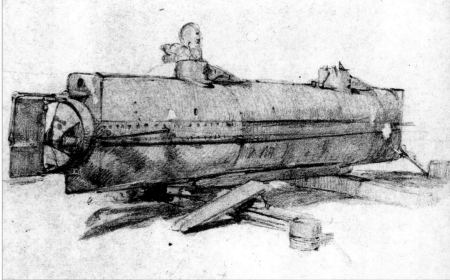

Previous pages left: The archival caption for this photo indicates that these Negroes are teamsters, photographed in 1864. The first reported use of blacks as laborers for the U.S. Army was as early as 1861, when Major General Benjamin Butler first applied the term "contraband of war" (meaning property legitimately seized from an enemy) to runaway slaves who entered his camp in Virginia. By 1862 Congress authorized the use of blacks in the war effort, and of course on January 1, 1863, the Emancipation Proclamation went into effect and large numbers of Negroes were recruited.

Previous pages top right: According to official figures, 179,000 Negroes served in the armies and navies of the United States during the Civil War. Countless others were utilized by field commanders to help construct fortifications, build bridges, and for other manual labor. The complete contribution of blacks to the war effort can never be known, but there was indeed an impact on the ultimate Union victory.

Previous pages bottom right: One of the oddest contraptions to see naval service was the Confederate submarine *H.L. Hunley,* named for its inventor, who lost his life in the vessel on a diving run in October 1863. Several accidents involving the *Hunley* and its trial runs cost the lives of many crew members, who must have been daring, adventuresome sorts just to be associated with such a novelty. The *Hunley's* moment of fame occurred on the evening of February 17, 1864, when it sank the sloop USS *Housatonic* near Charleston, South Carolina. The *Hunley* and her crew were lost in the victory.

Opposite top: These black troops are convalescing at Aiken's Landing on the James River in late 1864. Whether they are recovering from battle wounds or bouts of disease is not known. It is a fact, though, that black troops were used during the Petersburg siege, and in actions by the Army of the James, under Ben Butler, in the summer of 1864.

Opposite bottom: With the influx of blacks into the service, many wondered whether these new recruits would ever see action. Or would they be relegated to menial tasks and manual labor? Would they be brought out only on occasion to parade their freedom before the international community? True, a good many served garrison duty, releasing white units for front line service, but enough blacks saw action in over 400 engagements to incur a loss of 2,750 battle deaths and an untold number of wounded. Several black soldiers were awarded the Medal of Honor for conspicuous valor in battle. An estimated 29,000 members of the U.S. Colored Troops died of disease.

Below: Civil War prisons gained a ghastly notoriety in 1864 as the Union halted prisoner exchanges and prison populations swelled. This structure, formerly the establishment of Libby & Son, Ship Chandlers & Grocers, of Richmond, Virginia, was converted to a prison to house captive Federal officers and was named simply Libby Prison. The three-story building was divided into eight large rooms. Of great escapes, Libby had its dramatic moments. After a long and involved process of digging a 50-foot tunnel and planning a breakout, 109 officers escaped on the night of February 9, 1864. Fifty-nine eventually reached Union lines.

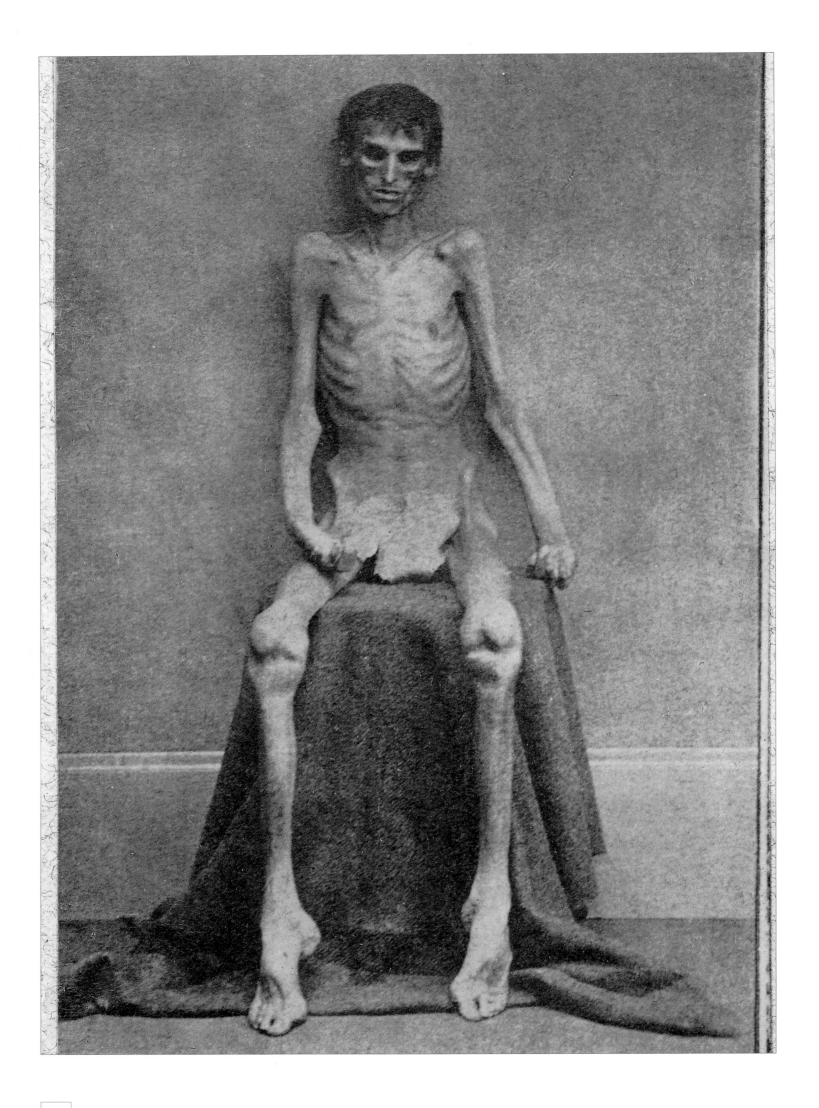

Previous pages left: This man should not be alive. He was released from Andersonville in this condition, and it was photographs such as this – he is undoubtedly one of the worst cases – that put the noose around Henry Wirz's neck. Heated debates still rage over the conditions at Andersonville. There should be no excuses, no apologies offered. No one can adequately defend this, and a condemnation is too easy. The last word on Andersonville should be its lesson to posterity.

Previous pages top right: This photograph of the Andersonville pen shows how crowded it was. There were no barracks, the water supply was inadequate, toilet facilities were primitive and insufficient, and the smell drifted on the breeze for miles. Originally comprising about 16-17 acres, the prison was later expanded to 26 acres, not all of which could be considered "living space" because of the swampy area used for sinks (toilet facilities). But even with the expansion, the prison was far too small for the 35,000 or so captives held there in August 1864, when deaths were greatest.

Previous pages bottom right: No Civil War prisoner ever walked away upon his release and had great things to say of his life in captivity – about the wonderful living conditions, the good food, and the doting attention of his "hosts." It was simply not a pleasant experience, North or South, and most memoirs of prison experience sound the same. But by far the worst prison of the war was the Confederate prison camp at Andersonville in southwestern Georgia. Many factors contributed to the deplorable conditions at the prison: supply shortages, the unexpectedly large number of prisoners to accommodate, and so on. It doesn't matter, for whatever the cause it existed, and men died by the thousands. Southerners were not barbarians, and prison officials attempted to explain that they did their best under the circumstances. They did not intentionally make Andersonville the hell-hole it became. But it happened, and 13,000 Federal enlisted men died there. Inevitably someone had to pay, and the Federal government hanged Commandant Henry Wirz after the war.

Bottom left: Where the care of doctors ended, at least for Union soldiers, the humanitarian care of the U.S. Sanitary Commission took over. A civilian organization founded in 1861, it was largely an all-volunteer outfit comprised of prominent doctors and other professionals, and funded by contributions. The commission performed a wide variety of services to men in the field, from providing pens and paper, stamps and other minor necessities, to operating field hospitals, ambulance service, and special care.

Bottom right: This soldier, identified on the archival caption as a medical director of hospitals, faced an enormous responsibility during the war. It has been estimated that for every soldier killed in battle or dead of a mortal wound, three died of disease. In 1864 and into 1865, deaths in prisons impacted mortality rates. All told, some 30,000 Union soldiers died in Confederate prisons, nearly half of that figure at Andersonville, and from 26,000-31,000 Confederate soldiers died in Union prisons.

Opposite: These men, photographed by the Brady company at Fredericksburg, Virginia, in May 1864, have had their lives drastically changed by the war. Arms and legs are missing, some are flat on their backs, others are sitting in quiet resolve. They appear to be the photographer's captive audience, and perhaps don't much care. Their thoughts are probably far away from the war. Who will bale the hay, now that I've lost my arm? Will my sweetheart leave me for another, whose legs are whole?

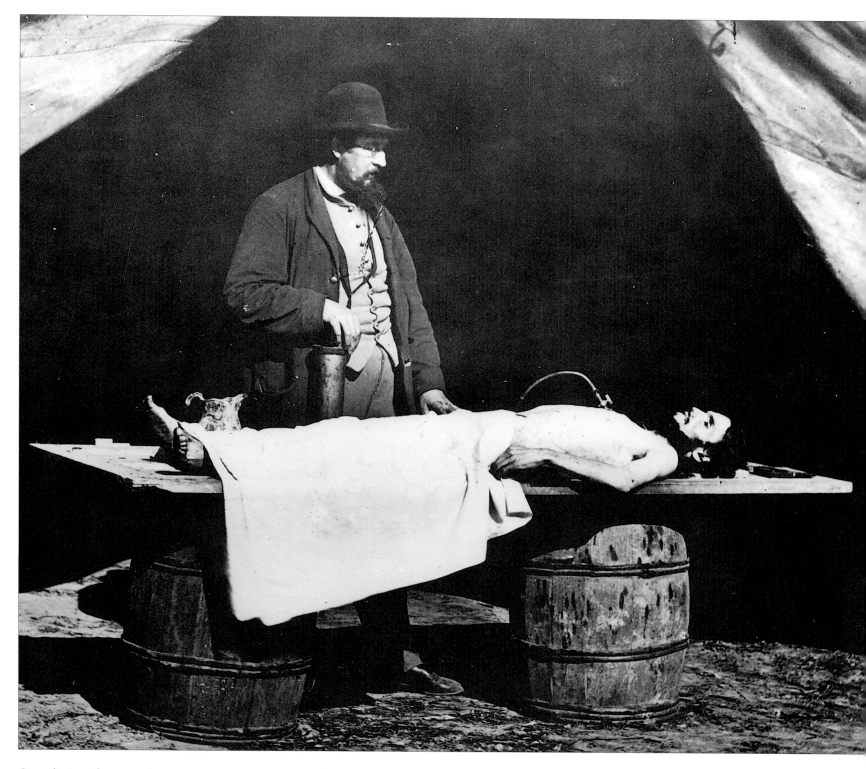

Opposite top: These convalescents were photographed by James Gardner (Alexander's brother) at the U.S. Sanitary Commission depot in Fredericksburg on May 20, 1864. They are men of Major General John Sedgwick's Sixth Corps, wounded at Spotsylvania. The general himself was killed by a sharpshooter's bullet on May 9. Known affectionately as "Uncle John" to his men, he'll always be remembered for his famous last words. While inspecting his lines at Spotsylvania, on foot, his aides told him that he was recklessly making a target of himself. He replied that "they couldn't hit an elephant at this distance." Seconds later a bullet struck him under the left eye and killed him.

Opposite bottom: War creates opportunity. Photographers sold thousands of images. Over 400 bordellos sprouted up in Washington alone. And Dr. Bunnell turned a dollar embalming the dead. Bereaved family and friends could take heart that once the deceased was taken behind the dirty canvas and treated by Dr. Bunnell, the body would be "free from odor or infection."

Above: The fact that this man is on an embalming table – assuming he's really dead, and not just posing for the camera – is evidence that he's far more fortunate than many other comrades who gave their lives for the cause. This man will no doubt be buried in a box of some sort with a headboard to mark his grave. Many others in this war were treated less delicately. The simple rule was that it was best to die in a battle your side won. That way you'd probably get a decent burial by your comrades or maybe even get embalmed and sent home for interment. If you died in a losing battle, on the other hand, and the enemy buried you, it was probably in a mass grave, your body tumbled in on top of many others, your identity known only to God.

Above: He was already famous as an actor. After April 1865, John Wilkes Booth (1838-1865) would be infamous as an assassin. He was born in Maryland into a family of accomplished actors, including his father Junius Brutus Booth, and brothers Edwin and Junius, Jr. The family loved Shakespeare's works, especially plays like *Julius Caesar*, where an assassin-hero rose up on behalf of the people to strike down a tyrant. Such ideals had been instilled in John Wilkes Booth since he was a boy. Because of the Lincoln administration's harsh measures in regard to the suspension of civil liberties during the war, such as suspending the writ of *habeas corpus*, and instituting martial law in Baltimore and other areas of strong secession sentiment, including Booth's home, the president appeared to Booth as a 19th-century Caesar.

Opposite top: Wilmington, North Carolina, was the last port still operating for the Confederacy. The city was guarded by Fort Fisher, and General Grant wanted the port closed. Beginning on Christmas Eve 1864, the fort came under heavy naval bombardment. The next day troops under Ben Butler landed in a dismally-unsuccessful attempt to storm the fort. Grant relieved Butler and planned another expedition, again using the fleet of Admiral David Dixon Porter to shell the fort, but the land forces were entrusted to Major General Alfred H. Terry. Operations recommenced on January 13, 1865, and Fort Fisher fell to the Federals on the 15th. Timothy O'Sullivan took this photo of the captured fort.

Opposite bottom: Commander of the Confederate garrison at Fort Fisher was Colonel William Lamb. On December 24, 1864 he and his men endured a severe bombardment from Porter's Union fleet. Then, on January 13, in what was said to represent the greatest firepower in naval history to that date, Porter's 627 guns opened again on the garrison. Some 20,000 projectiles rained down on Fort Fisher for three days. This drawing by Joseph Becker shows Confederate wounded being treated at a makeshift hospital in a bombproof.

Above: On January 21, 1865, General William T. Sherman left Savannah and officially transferred his headquarters to Beaufort, South Carolina. This was two days after his orders set his army in motion from Savannah. The march into South Carolina took on the appearance of a punitive expedition, as many of the Federals looked upon the state as the cradle of secession, the reason for the last four years of suffering and death. Beaufort, situated on the coast, had been in Union hands since 1861. This photograph shows the city transformed into a military post.

Opposite: On Sunday, March 4, 1865, Abraham Lincoln gave his second inaugural address from the steps of the Capitol. So long as the South chose to prosecute the war, Lincoln vowed to fight them to the last drop of blood. But once hostilities ceased, the president hoped to bring the wayward states quickly back to the fold. His inauguration speech stressed a policy of conciliation for the South: "With malice toward none; with charity for all; ... let us strive ... to bind up the nation's wounds ... to do all which may achieve and cherish a just, and a lasting peace ...." The president had six weeks to live.

Above: This photograph of captured Petersburg was probably taken a week after the Union occupation (according to a recent study of campaign images) by cameraman John Reekie, an employee of Alexander Gardner. Often mislabeled, probably for dramatic purposes, as the "first" Federal wagon train to enter the city, it is actually a photograph of one of many Union wagon trains leaving town, likely on April 10, exiting by way of Washington Street.

Opposite top: The time had come for the Confederates to evacuate Richmond. There was a mad dash to gather or destroy government documents and the Confederacy took flight. Jefferson Davis and cabinet members left Richmond by train on the night of April 2. There was pandemonium in the streets. Nothing should be left to the conquerors. Out on the James River, as depicted in this lithograph, gunboats were destroyed, the resulting explosions rocking the capital city only a few miles away.

Opposite bottom: This sketch depicts Duryee's New York Zouaves marching down Sycamore Street in Petersburg. The namesake of Abram Duryee, who ended the war a major general, his Zouaves were officially mustered in as the 5th New York Infantry in 1861. Patterned after the old French army, the Zouaves wore brightly-colored uniforms, complete with gaiters, baggy pants, short jacket and a turban, of sorts. The unit was organized in New York City in May 1861, and participated in most of the major battles of the Army of the Potomac until May 1863, when it was mustered out upon expiration of its term of service. Members with time yet to serve were assigned to the 146th New York Infantry, the official designation for the unit that marched down Sycamore Street in April 1865.

Opposite: At the time of the Civil War, according to census records, Richmond, Virginia was the 25th largest city in the United States, with 38,000 people. As evidence of population disparities North and South, Richmond was the third largest Southern city, behind New Orleans (169,000) and Charleston, South Carolina (41,000). In the North, New York City alone had 806,000 inhabitants, and well over a million if Brooklyn were added. Washington had a population of 61,000. When Richmond became the capital of the Confederacy in 1861, many predicted the very scene pictured here, taken in Richmond in 1865 by Brady & Company.

Above: On Sunday morning, April 2, President Jefferson Davis was attending services at St. Paul's Episcopal Church in Richmond when news arrived that the time had come to give up Petersburg and Richmond. The Yankees had broken through! The end came quickly.

Right: It had been the target of every commander of the Army of the Potomac. "On to Richmond!" was the battle cry. McClellan had gotten the closest in 1862 during his Peninsula Campaign. But then Robert E. Lee took command of the Army of Northern Virginia and slapped "Little Mac" back down the Peninsula to his boats. Then came boastful John Pope who, while he didn't command the Potomac army, did lead the force that was defeated in the Second Bull Run Campaign, which soon became part of the enlarged army that McClellan ultimately turned over to Ambrose Burnside. Under the latter's leadership, Richmond was made to appear even more out of grasp when he led the army to its most fruitless and deadly affair at Fredericksburg. Next came confident Joe Hooker – and embarrassment and defeat at Chancellorsville. When Richmond finally fell, Grant and Meade were in command, and the passage through the capital city of the Confederacy was swift and without fanfare. They were in pursuit of a more important target – Lee's army. Pictured here is long-elusive Richmond, with ordnance strewn about the riverfront, and the lonely capitol building in the distance.

Previous pages : During the mass exodus of troops, government workers, frightened citizens, and anyone else who had reason to fear the oncoming legions of Abraham Lincoln, the roads were clogged with traffic, all heading west, away from the Yankees. Through the night of April 2 into the early hours of the 3rd, fear and dashed hopes marked the procession. Sometime around three o'clock in the morning a fire started that soon spread to adjacent structures, and in a short time the flames were roaring out of control, consuming much of the capital. This was several hours before the Federals arrived in Richmond, and what they found was a smoldering city. One of the earliest visitors to the conquered capital was Lincoln himself, who sat in Jeff Davis' chair within hours of the capture of the city. Alexander Gardner took this photograph of Richmond in ruins on April 6.

Below: At the outbreak of war Richmond was a prosperous city. Trade was at a high level, and with the prosperity came social and cultural advances. Richmond led the South in manufacturing and milling, producing great quantities of iron, flour, tobacco, and other principal commodities. Of primary note, Richmond's Tredegar Iron Works produced about a thousand cannons during the war, as well as plating for ironclads. Operations expanded into the production of gun carriages, shoes, and bricks. Employment swelled from 900 to 2,500 workers by 1863. Heading the operations at Tredegar was Brigadier General Joseph R. Anderson, who had taken the field early in the war, but returned to run Tredegar, his greatest service to the Confederacy. This photograph shows all sorts of ordnance scattered about the yard of Tredegar Iron Works after the evacuation of Richmond.

Opposite: Other places were left in ruins. In South Carolina, many Charleston residents were certain that their city, where the war had begun, would be plundered and burned. To avoid the loss of valuables and cherished personal items, and some public property, such as the bells of St. Michael's Church, Charlestonians had shipped the goods to the state capital at Columbia for safe-keeping. As fate would have it, Sherman by-passed Charleston and arrived at Columbia in February 1865. Pictured here are the ruins of the city. Sherman claimed he never gave an order to burn the capital.

Left: When Lee was finally outflanked and pushed back at Petersburg, he knew that he must evacuate both the area and the capital – which he did on April 3. He had hoped to break out to the southwest to join with Johnston's troops in North Carolina, however, harried by Sheridan's cavalry, and desperately short of supplies, he was forced to head off in a more westerly direction, causing his already slender army to wither away at an alarming rate. The intention had been to feed the hungry and weary men from the four supply trains at Appomattox station, but when the vanguard arrived they found Sheridan's men already in possession and the trains burned. With no way out of the trap and his army reduced to just 13,000 men, Lee was forced to accept Grant's terms of surrender. The illustration at left, reproduced from *Harper's Weekly*, purports to show the surrender being announced to Lee's army.

Above: The end came on Palm Sunday, April 9, 1865 at Appomattox Court House, Virginia. In the parlor of Wilmer McLean's house, Lee came to terms with Grant and the Civil War was effectively over. Ironically, McLean had lived near Manassas in 1861, where his residence was damaged during the first major battle of the war. He and his family moved to Appomattox, which they considered to be outside the war zones. It is an oft-repeated anecdote that the war started in McLean's front yard and ended in his parlor. This famous sketch shows General Lee, mounted on his favorite horse Traveller, riding away from McLean's, followed by the general's aide, Colonel Charles Marshall. Watching from the roadside and the steps of the house are awed Union soldiers. McLean's house was soon stripped for souvenirs by Federal officers.

Right: Now that the shooting was over, all that remained was the paperwork. Paroles had to be printed, so a press was brought in. An estimated 26,000 prisoners had to be processed at Appomattox. During the war, Robert Ould served the Confederacy as a commissioner on the Bureau of Exchange of Prisoners. According to the note attached to the document presented here, it was discovered among Ould's personal papers years after his death and loaned to the Confederate Museum in Richmond.

Below: As Lee's army retreated west toward Amelia Court House, where supplies were supposed to meet them, many men were unable to keep going. They were snatched up by Union cavalry in close pursuit of Lee's army, or were not quick enough in getting out of town and were trapped. Or they may simply have given up. These Rebels have lost hope, and in this sketch by Alfred Waud, made on the outskirts of Richmond, are seen taking the oath of allegiance to the United States.

Opposite: Lee's veterans could hardly believe it. Surrender! But they knew it must have been a last resort for Bobby Lee, their beloved commander, to admit defeat. Indeed, from the time the army evacuated Richmond and Petersburg it had been one disaster after another. Arriving at Amelia Court House on April 4, there were no supplies waiting for them. On April 6, at Sayler's Creek, about a fourth of the Army of Northern Virginia was cut off and captured. Then Federal cavalry raced ahead and seized Appomattox Station, blocking Lee's only escape route. This drawing shows Lee taking leave of his men after the surrender.

Above: On April 14, two days after the formal surrender ceremony at Appomattox, the Lincolns planned a night out at Ford's Theatre. A comedy was playing, *Our American Cousin*, starring Laura Keene. It was her 1000th performance. Booth was a familiar figure around Ford's and pretty much had the run of the place, having performed on its stage many times. The Lincolns had seen him perform there, and the president thought him quite good. Access to the president's box would be no problem for Booth. He planned to strike that night.

Right: On April 12 a formal surrender ceremony took place at Appomattox. The remnants of the proud Army of Northern Virginia marched up their final road. For the last time their battle-scarred banners were tossed to the breeze. There was no celebration on the part of the Yankees. In fact, the sides saluted one another in a solemn ceremony. The Confederates stacked their arms and furled their flags, then had a meal, compliments of the Federal government, and each man started home with a parole in his pocket. Grant's terms were lenient. Officers could keep their sidearms, horses and all personal baggage. Cavalrymen in Confederate service had provided their own mounts. Grant allowed the men to keep their horses, as they would be needed for the spring planting at home. As long as the terms of parole were adhered to, meaning that there would be no further taking up of arms against the United States, all could go home and live unmolested by the government.

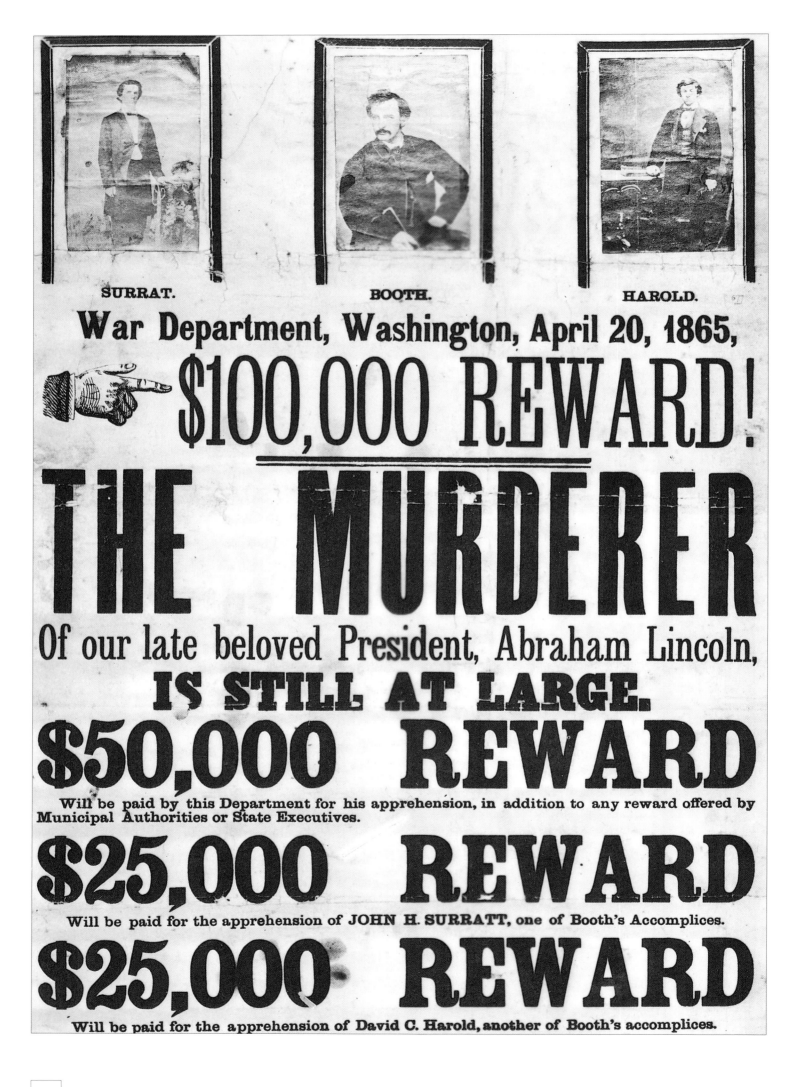

Previous pages left: Booth leaped from the box onto the stage before a startled audience, then made his escape out the back door of the theatre, mounted his horse and rode off into the night. He was recognized by many present in the theatre, and detectives soon had names of possible conspirators. The chase was quickly organized and wanted posters screamed out huge rewards. Meanwhile, the president died quietly just before seven-thirty on the morning of April 15, at a private residence across the street from Ford's Theatre.

Previous pages right: John Wilkes Booth was devastated by the surrender of Lee's army. He hated Lincoln and had for years, ever since the president declared martial law in Booth's home state of Maryland. Wholesale "arbitrary arrests" became the order of the day in Baltimore and other areas as the government ignored the writ of *habeas corpus* in an attempt to root out disloyalty where it existed. The measures were indeed harsh, as Lincoln himself would have admitted, but he had pledged to save the Union, and he had done just that. Booth viewed Lincoln as a tyrant, a dictator, a Caesar – and the young actor would take the real-life role of Brutus. This lithograph published in 1865 shows Booth's "accomplice."

Above left: Sam Arnold knew Booth as a kid and became a member of the conspiracy when its goal was to kidnap the president, not murder him. Arnold was a Georgetown graduate and a veteran of Confederate service. His interest in the new plot grew thin and on March 27, in a letter to Booth, Sam expressed his concerns. In effect, he wanted out, and he did bow out. It was his letter, though, found among Booth's effects, that connected him to the plot, and Arnold went to prison.

Above right: This man, George Atzerodt, was supposed to assassinate Vice President Andrew Johnson but never came close, probably because his heart was not in the project. He made his living running a small smuggling operation at Port Tobacco, Maryland, though his legitimate occupation was that of carriage painter. He was not a well man and was living with his mistress and their two-year-old daughter when he got involved with Booth. Originally, Booth intended to abduct the president, and Atzerodt was to help smuggle him into Virginia. Then the war ended, and Booth's scheme turned to assassination. A cavalry detail caught up with Atzerodt at his cousin's house in Maryland on April 20.

Opposite: General and Mrs. Grant had been invited to be the Lincolns' guests that evening, but they had begged off in order to visit their children in New Jersey. Besides, Mrs. Lincoln and the general's wife never did get along. Major Henry Rathbone, a veteran of the Army of the Potomac, brevetted for gallantry during Grant's Overland Campaign, now posted to Washington on administrative duties, and his fiancee, Clara Harris, socialite daughter of a New York senator, attended the theatre as the Lincolns' guests. This drawing shows an accurate seating arrangement in the president's box that evening, when a single shot rang out. Rathbone tried to stop the intruder but was stabbed in the arm by Booth.

Above: Booth's partner on the run was this man, David Herold, who, despite his derelict appearance, had attended Georgetown College and was not as stupid as history generally records. Herold met up with Booth in Maryland after each was fortunate enough to make his way past a bridge guard and out of Washington. Herold was with Booth when the assassin's end came at the Garrett farm on April 26, when a detachment from the 16th New York Cavalry caught up with the fugitives and Booth was mortally wounded.

Opposite: Edman "Ned" Spangler was a carpenter at Ford's Theatre and a long-time acquaintance of Booth. Spangler's only role in the assassination was an unwitting one. Before Booth made his way up to the president's box he asked Ned if he would mind holding his horse out back of the theatre for a moment or two. Ned was busy backstage and couldn't spare the time, but he called to a young helper named "Peanuts" to keep an eye on Booth's horse. Spangler was charged with aiding Booth's escape and received a prison sentence.

Left: An estimated 300 suspects were arrested in the assassination case. It was in many ways a "witch hunt," with a lot of people taken into custody because they resembled Booth. But by the beginning of May the government had decided who would face trial. They were David Herold, Samuel Arnold, George Atzerodt, Edman Spangler, Lewis Powell (his role in the plot was the unsuccessful murder attempt on Secretary of State William H. Seward, who was severely slashed with a knife but survived Powell's attack), Dr. Samuel A. Mudd (a Maryland physician who set Booth's broken leg, an injury probably caused when his horse fell on him, not in jumping from the president's box to the stage, as is generally believed), and Mary E. Surratt (who ran a boarding house in Washington where some of the alleged conspirators stayed or frequented, and she owned a tavern in the Maryland countryside where Booth stopped to pick up weapons during his escape). Mary's son John, a member of the Confederate "secret service," was also a suspect, but he avoided capture until months after the trial. The government moved swiftly, as is evidenced by this photograph taken on July 7, 1865. While the rest were given prison terms, Mary Surratt, Lewis Powell, David Herold and George Atzerodt (left to right on the gallows) met a different fate.

Left: The war was over, the South shattered and Lincoln dead from the assassin's bullet when the triumphant Union Army staged its last Grand Review down Pennsylvania Avenue. The review took place over two days, May 23-24, 1865, after which the men were mustered out of volunteer service to return home. Looking beyond the ranks of infantry marching to the strains of martial music, a contemporary reviewer noted that "Behind the glamor of military achievement lies the cruel cost to be compensated for only by the necessity for deciding the questions that had threatened the foundations of the American nation."

Above: Henry Wirz was born in Switzerland. Traveling to America in 1849 to avoid some difficulties in money matters, he claimed to be a physician. Conflicting accounts over his education make it difficult to determine for certain if he had formal training in medicine, but it is likely he did not, though he probably had experience in some capacity as a medical attendant of some sort. The verifiable record on Wirz begins with his enlistment in the 4th Louisiana. His earliest association with the Confederate prison system was in 1862 in Richmond, serving as a captain under Brigadier General John H. Winder, who did not live to the end of the war. By 1864 Wirz was a major in command of the Andersonville, Georgia prison camp. This photograph was taken on the day of his execution, November 10, 1865, after conviction on the charge of war crimes against prison inmates. His guilt or innocence is still passionately debated.

Opposite: Succeeding to the presidency upon Lincoln's death was Vice President Andrew Johnson (1808-1875), also a target of Booth's conspiracy, but assigned to an unwilling assassin. Born in North Carolina, he moved as a teenager to Greeneville, Tennessee with his parents. Largely self-educated, Johnson served as governor of Tennessee and later U.S. Senator. He remained loyal to the United States, and as the appointed war governor of Tennessee he ruled with a firm hand, earning many enemies in his home state. As the 17th President, Johnson attempted to follow through with the policies of Reconstruction that Lincoln had outlined, but the Radical Republicans thought him too lenient on the South. In 1868 he narrowly missed conviction in impeachment proceedings.

Opposite: Finally at home, at the Richmond house the Confederate government provided, is Robert E. Lee, who allowed the Brady company to take this photograph on Easter Sunday, April 16, a week after Appomattox. Mathew Brady himself claimed credit for arranging the session, through Colonel Robert Ould. Flanking the general on his right is son George Washington Custis Lee, himself a major general, and the other man is Lieutenant Colonel Walter Taylor, Lee's trusted adjutant who was with him the entire war.

Overleaf left: Jefferson Davis was captured in Georgia in May 1865. He spent two years imprisoned at Fortress Monroe while the government decided what to do with him. Any other country would have hanged him. Finally he was released, and was never prosecuted for anything. He settled near Biloxi, Mississippi and wrote *The Rise and Fall of the Confederate Government*, published in 1881. He's pictured here with his wife Varina after the war. Jefferson Davis died in 1889.

Overleaf right: The most enduring symbol of the Lost Cause was Robert E. Lee. Several months after Appomattox he moved to Lexington, Virginia and accepted the presidency of Washington College, now Washington and Lee University. The small college, hurt by the war like so many other similar institutions, prospered again with a man of Lee's stature at the helm. He died in 1870, of heart disease, the early signs of which had plagued him during the Civil War. Lee is buried in the chapel he had built on the Washington College campus.

Below: The cost was heavy. Deaths in the Union armies and navies were estimated at over 360,000, the largest share attributed to loss of life from disease. The number of wounded was placed at 275,000, though this is a dubious statistic because many men were wounded more than once. Of the more unusual causes of death were the 520 listed as murdered, 4,944 who drowned, and 267 listed as executed by the government. On the Confederate side, it is much more difficult to arrive at casualty figures due to incomplete or non-existent records. But experts in the field of "educated guessing" place the number of dead at 258,000, and those wounded at 194,000. Combined deaths, North and South, thus can be estimated at over 600,000. Neither of the armies' figures take into account war-related civilian deaths, an impossible figure to conjure up, but no doubt a significant number. Pictured here is a cemetery in Alexandria, Virginia, photographed by Brady.

Opposite: The war was over, but not everybody could go home. The South had lost, and feelings were still bitter. In order to help keep peace in the once-rebellious cities of the South, a military presence had to remain for some time. It was all part of the greater concept of the dirty word "Reconstruction." As bad as it was, it could have been worse. This scene in the streets of New Orleans during postwar occupation captures some of the problems of the day: soldiers arguing with civilians; blacks, now free, not quite sure what their new station in life meant; the fellows at lower left appear to be business types, perhaps "Carpetbaggers" or worse, "Scalawags," plotting some new financial venture to aid the rebuilding of the South, but mainly to line their own pockets.

Below: Change would come slow, or not at all in some parts of the reunited nation. Spawned by Reconstruction, secret societies like the Ku Klux Klan were established in the South to preserve white interests. Negroes comprised a huge percentage of the Southern population, over 50 percent in some states. When blacks were granted full citizenship in 1868 and the right to vote in 1870, ill feelings only intensified, especially among middle class Southern whites, many of whom had lost everything in the war. The Klan, with its rituals and costumes, and its goal of upholding the rights of whites, became an outlet of expression – oftentimes violent – for many Southerners. One of the early leaders of the Ku Klux Klan was Confederate General Nathan Bedford Forrest.

Opposite: It was time now to convert from a wartime to a peacetime economy. If the nation was truly to bind up its wounds, North and South had to work together. And what better arena for the soothing of wounds to begin than in the economic sphere? Socially, it would take some time. Culturally, the South was too stricken. Economically, sectional prejudices could be set aside if there was a dollar to be made. Here at the Cincinnati, Ohio waterfront shortly after the war, with the Kentucky hills in the background, where elements of Bragg's Confederate army had appeared in 1862, commerce could begin once the debris of war was cleared away from the dock.

Below: This Thomas Nast sketch in 1872, entitled "One Vote Less," shows to what lengths some Klansmen would go in order to "protect their interests." Activities ran the gamut from frightening Negroes from voting to outright murder. The original principles adopted by the Ku Klux Klan were: to protect the weak and oppressed; to defend the Constitution of the United States; and to protect the people from unlawful seizure and trial except by their peers. No one could argue with any of these goals. None seems to explain the reason for Nast's murder victim. Not every victim was a Negro. Carpetbaggers and Scalawags were also targets. By 1871, when President Hayes withdrew occupation troops from the South, the original Ku Klux Klan had mostly disbanded.

THE AFTERMATH OF WAR

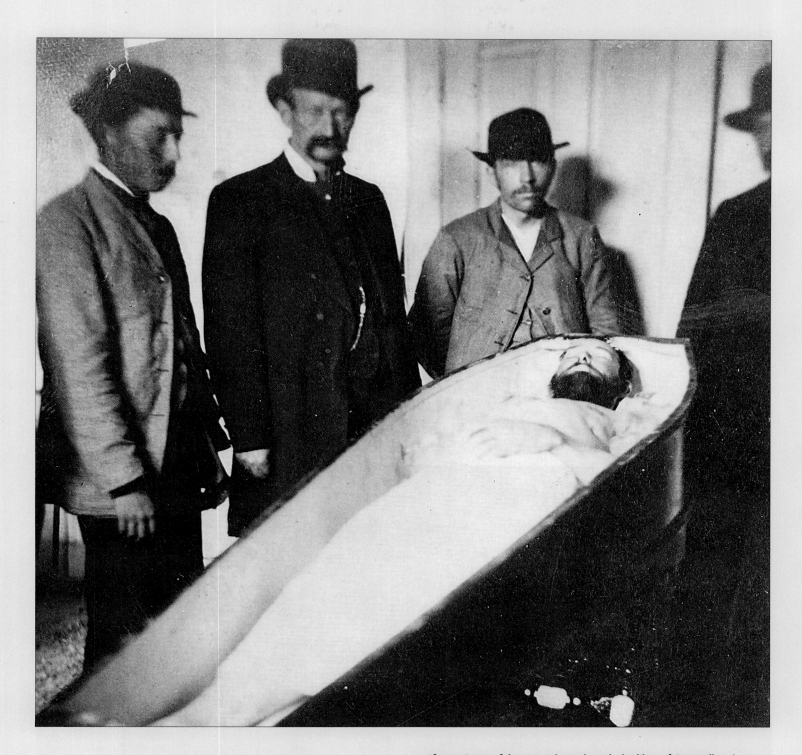

Above: Some of the men who rode with the likes of Quantrill and Anderson – neither of whom survived the war – and gained fame as outlaws in the two decades after the Civil War, were Frank and Jesse James, the Younger brothers, Clell Miller, just to name a few. Most ended up like Jesse James, shown here, propped up to be photographed in death. In 1882 he was shot by Bob Ford, a member of Jesse's gang, when his back was turned. Indeed, much of the lawlessness of the Old West stemmed from unfinished business in the Civil War.

Opposite: There was killing along the Kansas-Missouri border nearly a decade before the Civil War. Free-staters and pro-slavery men clashed over the Kansas-Nebraska Act of 1854 to the extent that the term "Bleeding Kansas" emerged into common usage. The Civil War merely intensified and broadened the conflict in the region. Bushwhackers in Missouri gave no quarter, and expected none in return, as they murdered Yankees in the name of the Confederacy, but mostly out of a personal cause of hatred and vengeance. Guerrilla leaders such as William Clarke Quantrill and "Bloody Bill" Anderson added a unique chapter to the Civil War. Union soldiers captured by these cutthroats were generally killed on the spot. Sometimes their scalps were lifted. The young man pictured here rode with Bloody Bill late in the war. His name: Jesse James, whose war did not end with Appomattox.